M000240170

SO YOU WANT TO BE A LAWYER

THE ULTIMATE GUIDE TO GETTING INTO AND SUCCEEDING IN LAW SCHOOL

Skyhorse Publishing

Copyright © 2012 by Timothy B. Francis, Esq., Lisa Jones Johnson, Esq., and Walter C. Jones, Esq.

The fact pattern is a work of fiction. It is not meant to depict, portray, or represent any particular gender, real persons, or group of people. All characters, incidents, and dialogue are products of the authors' imagination and are not to be construed as real. Any resemblance to actual events or persons, living or dead, is purely coincidental.

The legal principles, statements, and legal conclusions set forth in this book are offered for the purposes of teaching only and should not be construed as binding statements of law.

THE ANATOMY OF A CRIME: THE FACTS are taken from the screenplay "Ivy League," Copyright © 1992 and "Still Waters," Copyright © 1993, registered with the Writers Guild-West by Timothy B. Francis Esq. & Lisa Jones Johnson Esq. used with permission.

THE ANATOMY OF A CRIME: BONUS PROBLEM is taken from the screenplay "Lucid Interval," Copyright © 1991, registered with the Writers Guild-West by Lisa Jones Johnson, Esq. & Timothy B. Francis, Esq., used with permission.

All Rights Reserved. No part of this book may be reproduced in any manner without the express written consent of the publisher, except in the case of brief excerpts in critical reviews or articles. All inquiries should be addressed to Skyhorse Publishing, 307 West 36th Street, 11th Floor, New York, NY 10018.

Skyhorse Publishing books may be purchased in bulk at special discounts for sales promotion, corporate gifts, fund-raising, or educational purposes. Special editions can also be created to specifications. For details, contact the Special Sales Department, Skyhorse Publishing, 307 West 36th Street, 11th Floor, New York, NY 10018 or info@skyhorsepublishing.com.

Skyhorse® and Skyhorse Publishing® are registered trademarks of Skyhorse Publishing, Inc.®, a Delaware corporation.

www.skyhorsepublishing.com

10 9 8 7 6 5 4 3 2 1

Library of Congress Cataloging-in-Publication Data is available on file.

ISBN: 978-1-62087-209-3

Printed in the United States of America

Praise for

SO YOU WANT TO BE A LAWYER

**Empowerment through awareness,
So You Want to be a Lawyer is challenging and enlightening,
a must read for the aspiring law student.**
Debra Martin Chase, Producer of the *Princess Diaries*,
The Sisterhood of the Traveling Pants and *the Cheetah Girls* movie franchises. Mount Holyoke
College and Harvard Law School graduate.

***So You Want to be a Lawyer* is the handbook for anyone who
wants to succeed and thrive in law school and beyond.**
James Garner, JD, Tulane University, 1989, Order of the Coif,
Magna Cum Laude, Managing Editor of the *Tulane Law Review*, no. 63.

**If you're thinking about law school,
do yourself a favor, read this book first.**
Everett Bellamy, Senior Assistant Dean for the JD Program and Adjunct Professor of
Law at Georgetown University Law Center.

**Brilliant and innovative, the authors capture the essence
of the legal experience in one fell swoop, bravo!**
Marc H. Morial, Esq., President and CEO of the National Urban League.
BS University of Pennsylvania, and JD, Georgetown University Law Center, 1983.

The handbook for every prospective law student.
Pascal Calogero Jr., former Chief Justice of the Louisiana Supreme Court

**A true act of generosity, I wish this book had been available
when I was thinking of going to law school.**
Nancy J. Taylor, Esq., University of California at Berkeley
School of Law. *California Law Review,* 1987

***So You Want to be a Lawyer* is a dynamic approach
to understanding the mechanics of law school and testing
your potential for success in law school.**
Antoinette C. Bush, Partner at Skadden, Washington D.C.
Wellesley College and Northwestern University School of Law graduate.

THIS BOOK IS FOR YOU
IF YOU...

1. WANT AN INSIDE LOOK AT THE STUDY AND PRACTICE OF LAW
2. ARE THINKING ABOUT BECOMING A LAWYER AND WANT TO MAKE AN INFORMED DECISION ON WHAT TO STUDY IN COLLEGE
3. WANT ASSISTANCE ON HOW TO SELECT A LAW SCHOOL
4. WANT TO BETTER UNDERSTAND THE LAW SCHOOL ADMISSIONS PROCESS
5. WANT THE NAMES AND ADDRESSES OF A.B.A. APPROVED LAW SCHOOLS AND INFORMATION ABOUT FINANCIAL ASSISTANCE
6. WOULD LIKE TO ENHANCE YOUR CHANCES FOR ADMISSION TO LAW SCHOOL
7. WOULD LIKE A HEAD START OVER OTHER FIRST YEAR LAW STUDENTS
8. WOULD LIKE PRACTICE SOLVING LEGAL PROBLEMS THE WAY LAW STUDENTS DO IN LAW SCHOOL AND THE WAY A LAWYER MIGHT IN A COURTROOM
9. WOULD LIKE INFORMATION ABOUT CAREER OPPORTUNITIES AS A LAWYER
10. WANT THE ULTIMATE HANDBOOK ON THE STUDY AND PRACTICE OF LAW

SO YOU WANT TO BE A LAWYER

THE ULTIMATE GUIDE TO GETTING INTO AND SUCCEEDING IN LAW SCHOOL

TABLE OF CONTENTS

To our children
*Alexandra, Brendon, Jarone,
Olivia, and Sara*

ABOUT THE AUTHORS

TIMOTHY B. FRANCIS is of counsel to the prestigious law firm of Sher Garner Cahill Richter Klein & Hilbert, LLC in New Orleans, Louisiana, where his practice is concentrated in areas of commercial litigation and business transactions. Mr. Francis received his BA from Xavier University in 1980 and his JD from Tulane University in 1984, where he served as president of his law school class. He resides in New Orleans, Louisiana.

LISA JONES JOHNSON is an attorney, author and entertainment executive. She is the CEO of NextGen Media Group, Inc. which recently launched a global social media platform focusing on news. In 2007, Ms. Johnson's debut novel *A Dead Man Speaks* (Genesis Press) was nominated for a 2007 Image Award and for the Romantic Times Literary Critics award for best general fiction. Ms. Jones Johnson is an honors graduate of Harvard College and the Harvard Law School, and she served as an adjunct professor of law at USC Law School where she taught a course on drafting and negotiating entertainment contracts. She resides in Los Angeles, California.

WALTER C. JONES is an attorney with extensive experience in business and finance transactions. He began his legal career at the Washington, D.C. office of Sidley & Austin after graduating in 1988 from Harvard Law School. Mr. Jones also worked as General Counsel at an asset-management firm where he was likewise responsible for all compliance matters. Mr. Jones earned his BA from Princeton University and the Woodrow Wilson School of Public and International Affairs, and his MBA from the George Washington University School of Business and Public Management. He resides in Washington, D.C.

FOREWORD

Like many people, I went to law school because I could not think of anything better to do. It was either law school or graduate school, and I figured that lawyers made more money. I liked to read, but I abhorred boredom. In fact, the fear of boredom made it difficult to accept the law as my best option. As a result, I was nonchalant and unprepared for what I walked into, and at first, overwhelmed by the law school experience. Looking back on it now, I only wish that I had been able to find an interesting way to get a look at what "the law" was all about before I was thrown into the rigors of the first year of law school.

So You Want to Be a Lawyer would have been beneficial because it takes an apparently boring subject and dissects it in a competent and entertaining way. On a fundamental level, the book addresses the basic question of, "How does a lawyer discover the truth?"

So You Want to Be a Lawyer is well presented and, should my son or daughter express an interest in pursuing a legal career, this is a book I would recommend. I would do so whether they were in high school, college, or had just been accepted to law school. *So You Want to Be a Lawyer* will reach readers at all three levels and will be of interest to a broad range of ages, maturity, and levels of interest. Advanced high school students, college students, and law students will all benefit from its unique approach to understanding the maze of intellectual hurdles that one must navigate to be a successful lawyer in the United States.

I am told that I am a decent lawyer, but my apparent competence is, more than anything else, a product of hard work. If *So You Want to Be a Lawyer* had been around at "the decision times" in my life, there is a good chance I would have read it and gotten a head start on where I am today. I would have paid attention to things that I had missed. I would have known what to look for. I think if I had read the book, I would be a better lawyer today.

As you can see, I am enthusiastic about this piece of work. I believe that it will help many students make informed decisions. It will make the law school experience more rewarding and supply the legal system with better lawyers. That is a lot to ask of any book, but this delightful exploration of "the law" is such a resource for anyone committed to the process of becoming an officer of the court.

Ronald Mason, Esq.
President, Southern University System
Columbia University
Columbia University School of Law

A NOTE ON ADVOCACY

Often times, when the topic of "the law" or "lawyers" is raised in discussion, a question is asked, "How can lawyers defend someone who is obviously guilty? Isn't that unethical? I just don't get it. If someone came into my office, confessed to a murder, and wanted to get off on a legal technicality, I wouldn't do it, would you?"

The answer lies in the nature of advocacy. Our legal system is based on the principle that everyone has a constitutional right to a fair trial and to legal representation. As officers of the court, lawyers are bound to zealously represent their clients and to ensure that they receive due process under the law.

All citizens of the United States of America have a constitutional right to competent legal representation, a right not based on the nature of the crime or on whether the defendant is guilty or innocent. Lawyers, as officers of the court, must be prepared to execute their duties with honesty, integrity, and competence.

The adversarial process is, in essence, a search for the truth with certain constitutional and evidentiary guidelines that the court must follow. Through the law school experience, we begin the journey of learning how to search for the truth in such an adversarial system.

Like other professions, lawyers have a choice in the area of law they decide to practice. However, in certain instances, courts assign lawyers cases. In cases where a lawyer feels that he or she cannot zealously represent their client, the attorney can petition the court to be excused.

Although lawyers are held to a higher standard than those who are not officers of the court, let us not forget that we all have a moral obligation as human beings to be honest and forthright. That is what true advocacy is all about: a search for truth and justice.

1 | HOW TO USE THIS BOOK

We suggest that you go through the book chronologically. Each section builds upon the skills that you will have tested in the previous section. The first part of the book will give you useful general information about law school, the admissions process, and careers in the law.

In the case briefing section, we: (1) explain how to brief a case; (2) give you a hypothetical criminal law case; and (3) provide a model brief for that case. We then give you actual cases from the first year law courses: Torts, Civil Procedure, Property, Contracts, and Constitutional Law. After each case is a space in which to write out your brief. Once you are finished briefing each case, there is a model brief for you to compare your answer. Remember, there is no one correct model answer. The model answers provided in this book specify the important information on which you should focus, and are only illustrative.

Take as much time as you need to brief the cases. The purpose of this section is to give you an opportunity to read and analyze actual legal decisions and to "dissect" each case. Moreover, remember, it is more important to make sure you understand each case before you begin briefing it than to worry about how long the whole process takes you.

In the section titled "Thinking Like a Lawyer," you will get a chance to test how well you understood the legal principles set forth by the judges in the five cases you briefed. You are given a summary of five fact patterns from five cases; cases on which you have just been briefed. You will then have to figure out which of the five cases would be cited for each of those sets of facts and why. After you have completed this exercise, you should check your answers against the holdings of the judges, provided at the end of this section.

Again, take as much time as you need for this part of the book. It tests an important skill that all lawyers must perfect—the ability to analyze a set of facts and determine which case law would apply to that particular fact pattern.

"The Anatomy of a Crime" gives you a chance to further test your analytical and reasoning skills against a complex fact pattern, but in this case, you will be applying statutory law to a set of facts, rather than case law as in the two previous exercises.

The statutory law that will apply to the fact pattern is set forth in the section titled "The Law." For this fact pattern, the statutory law will consist of various crimes, such as murder, assault, and battery.

Although you will no doubt have heard of some of these crimes, remember that the key to answering the questions correctly is not only to identify the crimes that have been committed, but also to be able to explain why defendants should be charged with these crimes. To do this, you will have to understand the elements of each of the crimes.

For instance, murder in the first degree has the following elements: intent to kill someone, pre-meditation, and the act of killing someone. If you believe murder in the first degree has occurred, you must explain how each of these elements is present in the fact pattern.

That's the essence of thinking as a lawyer—first identifying the applicable legal principal, in this case which crime may have been committed, and then identifying whether each element of the crime has, in fact, occurred in the fact pattern.

When you read "The Law," try to understand each crime, and then concentrate on each crime's element. If necessary, visualize the law as though someone were breaking it. This way you will remember it, rather than having to memorize it.

You will also find it easier to spot where a crime has occurred and logically explain why the defendant should be charged with this crime, based on how his or her actions correspond to each of the required elements of the crime.

Also, don't be afraid to read "The Law" several times and take notes. If you were a lawyer on a case, that is exactly what you would do! No one memorizes every detail of the law. On the contrary, lawyers read it repeatedly, take notes, and then determine which legal principles apply to their problem.

Let's discuss "The Facts." You will notice right away that they are not in a straight narrative format. We have done this to approximate the type of format you might face if you were a lawyer assigned to read a deposition. A deposition is an important tool lawyers use in preparing for a case.

In essence, it's a type of mini-trial without a judge or jury in which the lawyer asks a witness (usually in the presence of the witness' attorney) questions about the case. A court reporter records the witness' answers in much the same format that you will see in "The Facts." Therefore, when you begin to read this section, imagine you are a young lawyer who has been assigned to read the depositions (i.e. the answers or narration of the facts) being given by the witnesses and defendants in this case.

The key to getting a handle on "The Facts" is to distinguish between those sections that are relevant for determining whether a crime has been committed and those that are not. Don't be intimidated by the volume of material that you will have to read. Just remember that no matter what type of law you decide to practice, you will have to read a lot, so press on!

The questions that follow "The Facts" test whether you understand how to apply the law to those facts.

When you are answering the questions, remember that the reason a certain crime has been committed is as important as identifying the crime. Think about it like this: If you were a lawyer arguing before a judge or a jury, it would not be enough to say that the defendant had committed murder. You would have to prove that the defendant had committed the elements of the crime of murder.

Use common sense when answering the questions. Do not get so hung up on the mechanics of the law that you overlook the obvious. In other words, don't miss the forest for the trees. Remember, all laws are based on common sense applied in a logical way.

You will notice that the questions are of varying lengths and difficulty. In some cases, we have suggested time limits for each question, which generally correspond to the complexity of the question. We suggest that you attempt to stay within the time limits as much as possible to give yourself an accurate feel for what a law school exam would be like.

Model answers following each question will give you the correct answer to each question. In comparing your answers to those provided, remember to check whether your reasoning corresponds to the reasoning set forth in the correct answer.

That is one of the most important keys to thinking as a lawyer does—being able to reason logically. If you can do this, you have one of the most important skills needed for the study and practice of law. Remember, in the practice of law, there are always two sides to every question. Most cases are not "open and shut." The key to a successful defense of your position is how clearly, logically, and persuasively you can apply the law to your particular set of facts.

In conclusion, this is how we would suggest that you go through "The Anatomy of a Crime." First, read "The Law," taking notes on each of the crimes so that when you come across something in the facts that seems to correspond to one of the crimes, you will be able to identify it. Then read "The Facts." Take as long as you need with both sections. The key is to fully understand both before moving on to the questions. Then answer the questions and check each one against its model answer.

We are confident that after you have read *So You Want to Be a Lawyer,* you will have a good idea of the types of problem solving that lawyers face on a daily basis.

We hope you enjoy the book!

2 | PREPARING FOR LAW SCHOOL

Your Major

Unlike medical schools or other professional schools, law school does not require any specific major or concentration of study, although an undergraduate degree is usually required. While political science, economics, and English, are popular majors among many prospective law students (as is an interdisciplinary "pre-law" major offered by some colleges and universities), you'll find law students majoring in areas as diverse as engineering and fine arts.

It's more important to major in an area that you find interesting and rewarding and in which you can excel rather than majoring in something simply because it's popular among "prelaw" students.

Because the practice of law requires a variety of skills, it's important to have a well balanced education. For the personal injury lawyer, for instance, a working knowledge of anatomy can be helpful. So some science courses, although not necessary for the law school experience, may be helpful for the practice of law generally.

Also lawyers practicing personal injury or corporate law are often required to work with experts in various fields. Economists, for example, are frequently used in the calculation of future earnings of an individual or business.

Therefore, the successful lawyer must be able to converse competently with various experts. And what better place to learn the basics than in college? So don't blow off accounting, economics, or the sciences because you think they're too hard. In the long run they'll serve you well.

As for the business/corporate lawyer, individuals with specialized backgrounds can have a leg up on the competition if they have a specific skill. In fact, many companies with specialized areas of practice look for attorneys with an undergraduate degree in a technical field. For instance, an employer may require its patent lawyers to have a degree in chemistry or engineering.

The same is true for the pre-med major who decides to go to law school to practice medical malpractice law; he or she may have an advantage over someone who majored in music. Although specific majors aren't necessarily required for these positions, they give you an edge.

Keep in mind, however, that practical experience can be as important as an undergraduate major. For example, the former investment banker who goes to law school may ultimately have an advantage in getting a corporate securities job over an individual who has not. Once again, choosing a major that you enjoy and in which you can do well is of utmost importance.

The LSAT

The Law School Admissions Test, popularly known as the LSAT and administered by the Law School Admission Council in Princeton, New Jersey, is required for admission by most law schools. The LSAT is a standardized test designed to give law schools an idea of a prospective student's aptitude for the study of law. There are various LSAT preparatory courses which many people take prior to taking the LSAT.

There are also a number of LSAT preparation books which go over the same general material as the courses. Your scores on the LSAT are one of the key components that law schools use in determining admission. Also, doing well on the LSAT the first time you take it is important because law schools average the scores of people who take the test more than once. Thus some type of serious advance preparation is advisable to ensure the highest score possible.

Whether you take a course or use one of the preparation books depends on your finances (the courses can be expensive) and whether you find it more effective to learn on your own or in a classroom setting. However, whether it's a course or an LSAT prep book, we cannot overemphasize the importance of some type of preparation.

Generally you should take the LSAT during your junior year of college or the first semester of your senior year. Even if you're not planning to go to law school directly after college, you may still want to take the LSAT while you're still in college since it's often easier to prepare for the test while still in an academic environment.

If you've been out of college for a few years and you're considering law school, you should take the LSAT as soon as possible in order to ensure that you receive your scores in time to qualify for admission for the next academic year. For more information on the LSAT you can contact:

> Law School Admission Council 662
> Penn Street Newtown, PA 18940
> Telephone: (215) 968-1001
> Email: lsacinfo@LSAC.org
> www.lsac.org

For information on Opportunities for Minorities in the Law contact:

American Bar Association
The Commission on Racial and Ethnic
Diversity in the Profession
321 N Clark Street
Chicago, IL 60654
Email: minorities@americanbar.org
www.americanbar.org/groups/diversity/racial_ethnic_diver
sity.html

Diversity Initiatives Fund
662 Penn Street
Newtown, PA 18940
Telephone: (215) 968-1001
http://www.lsac.org/LSACResources/Grants/lsac-minority-
program-grants.asp

*For information regarding financing
your legal education you may contact:*

http://www.lsac.org/jd/finance/financial-aid-overview.asp

Improving Your Chances
of Being Accepted to Law School

If you don't have a strong undergraduate grade point average or
high LSAT scores, there are certain things that you can do to improve
your chances of being accepted to law school.

For instance, you may want to consider working for one or two
years before applying to law school. Ideally you should seek the type
of job that will enable you to hone your problem-solving skills, to
demonstrate your ability to work hard, and to show that you have a

mature attitude towards your work. These virtues are often lacking in college students.

In addition, working offers the opportunity to obtain favorable employer recommendations. The key is to give the law school admissions committees additional favorable information to offset your low grades and/or LSAT scores.

Some people may wonder about paralegal programs. Working as a paralegal gives you an idea of the law firm environment; however, law school admissions committees are more concerned with whether your work experience required reasoning and problem solving skills rather than simply that you worked in a law firm.

In addition, if you majored in an area that you would like to pursue after college, you may want to consider obtaining a masters degree in that area. Often, doing well in a masters program can be used by a law school admissions committee to show that you can do well in an academic environment. And although high grades in a masters program will not negate low undergraduate grades, they provide additional favorable information to improve the overall quality of your application.

If you come from an economically disadvantaged background, you may want to consider applying to CLEO, the Council on Legal Education Opportunity. CLEO is a federally funded summer program where graduating college seniors take first year law school classes with law professors. It's a six week program where you go full time to class, take exams, and receive grades and faculty evaluations. CLEO applications are available in the late winter of your senior year, and admissions decisions are usually made by the spring.

Successful completion of CLEO can help your law school application in two ways. First, if you've already applied to law school but have been wait-listed, you can write the admissions committee once you're admitted to CLEO and ask them to hold back on a final decision on your application until you've completed the program.

Once you've completed CLEO, you can send your grades and faculty evaluations to the law schools and ask them to consider those results as part of your application.

Second, if you have not yet applied to law school and you've decided to work for a year, you will have the results of the CLEO program to add to your law school admissions application when you apply to law school during September following your college graduation.

Finally, you may want to inquire with the local bar associations in your area to see if they have any summer or part-time pre-law programs. For example, in Washington D.C., The Charles Hamilton Houston Law School Preparatory Institute is a non-profit program that provides a summer pre-law program where participants take first-year law school classes with law professors and practicing attorneys. Like with CLEO, students are graded and receive faculty evaluations. Because the Institute is a non-profit organization, a minimal tuition is charged.

For more information on CLEO you can contact:

> Council on Legal Education Opportunity
> 740 15th St. NW
> 9th Floor
> Washington, D.C. 20005
> Telephone: (202) 828-6100
> Toll free: (866) 886-4343
> Email: cleo@americanbar.org
> www.cleoscholars.com

The Application Process

After deciding where you want to apply, write or call the admissions offices and request an application. Preferably, do this in August or September of the year *prior to* the academic year you would like to start law school.

Law schools with early admissions policies will let you know if you've been accepted in December or January if you have submitted a completed application (including LSAT scores and letters of recommendation) by a certain date, usually October or early November. Many law schools also have rolling admissions policies where they essentially fill their class on a first-come, first-served basis. Therefore, it's essential to get your application in as soon as possible.

Law school applications consist generally of one or more essays; two or more letters of recommendation from professors, academic advisors, and/or employers; basic information; and your LSAT scores. Currently, the Law School Data Assembly Service (LSDS), offered through the Law School Admission Council, handles most of the law school applications. Almost all ABA-approved law schools use LSDS as a method of standardizing law school application records. Some schools require applicants to process their entire application through the LSDS. Other schools require a separate, school-specific application in addition to the LSDS law report. Contact the specific schools to which you are applying to see what their application rules require. You can register for the LSDS at www.lsac.org.

The essay portion of the application is extremely important and should be taken very seriously, regardless of your grades or LSAT scores. Often, students with very high grades or LSAT scores short-change the essay and then wind up not being accepted at the schools of their choice. Generally, there are one or two lengthy (250 words or less) essays and several shorter essays. In some cases, the essay will simply ask you to write 250 words or less on any subject of your choosing. Alternatively, you may have to respond to specific questions.

The key to doing well on the essays is to demonstrate that you can write clearly, concisely, and fluidly. Since one of the most important skills a lawyer has is his or her ability to communicate in writing, law school admissions offices will be looking very carefully to see if you have that aptitude.

If you're able to write on a subject of your choosing, you may want to take a position on something and argue your position convincingly. Again, the ability to construct a persuasive argument is another key skill for a lawyer. The extent to which you can demonstrate that ability on your essay, the greater your chances will be of being accepted to the school of your choice.

The essay can also be an opportunity to explain any weak points in your application or any extenuating or unusual circumstances in your background.

Consider, for instance, that your grade point average is higher than your LSAT scores, and you traditionally do not do well on standardized tests. The essay would be an opportunity for you to explain to the admissions committee that you generally do not do well on standardized tests and thus do not feel as if your LSAT scores accurately reflect your ability to do well in law school. Therefore, you may argue that your LSAT scores should not receive as much weight as your grades in evaluating your application.

If you worked full or part time while in college, mention it, since you obviously would not have had as much time to devote to studying as students who did not work. Furthermore, if you come from an economically disadvantaged background and have had to overcome considerable obstacles to attend college, you may also want to mention those circumstances.

In addition, mention any extracurricular activities you were in charge of or that had a particular impact on your school or community. In short, treat the essay like an interview in which you have the opportunity to tell the admissions committee anything about your background or experiences that would make them view your application more favorably.

Remember that an admissions committee will be reading countless applications. Many of these applications will say virtually the same things and the applicants will have almost indistinguishable credentials. To stand out and make the committee want you, it's important to distinguish yourself convincingly and articulately from the crowd, even if you have great grades and a high LSAT score.

Another important essay issue is length. If the application requests an essay of 250 words or less, you should not write 260 words. Because law school admissions offices read thousands of applications, they do not appreciate essays that exceed their prescribed word limits. Remember, concise writing is essential. After you've completed a rough draft of your essay, have a professor, friend, parent, or someone whose writing you respect critique it for you.

Someone once said that the essay should be your best piece of writing ever, and that is no exaggeration. Spend as much time as you need writing and re-writing your essay. You only get one bite out of the apple, so you want to make it your best effort.

Most, if not all, of the top law schools consider a number of other factors before they decide whom to admit. For example, they'll take affirmative steps to ensure that their student body represents a cross section of the population.

Accordingly, they may accept a student from Spokane, Washington, with the same or a slightly lower grade point average over another student from New York City if the freshman class is primarily New Yorkers.

A student who worked full time and had extracurricular activities may receive additional consideration over another student who may have had slightly higher grades, but no extracurricular activities. In either case, law schools don't accept students who they don't believe have the aptitude or drive to succeed at their institution.

A word to the wise: Apply to more than one school and have one or two "safety" schools where you're confident of being accepted.

Selecting a Law School

As previously mentioned, it's important to apply to more than one law school. We suggest at least four, but no more than ten (unless you want to spend a small fortune on application fees).

But the question remains, how do you decide to which law schools to apply? To get you started, a list of ABA-approved law schools and the addresses of their admissions office are in the appendix of this book. Now, how do you determine from that list where you should apply, particularly if you're only familiar with the better-known schools? What about the others?

We suggest you consider the following factors. First, decide whether you plan to attend law school full time or part time. Many law schools offer a night program for those who choose to work a full-time day job. However, if you enroll in a night program, it will usually take four years rather than three to finish law school.

Next, ask yourself where you ultimately want to practice law. If it's in your home state or town, you may want to seriously consider the local schools in your area. Many of the attorneys in that area will have come from those schools, and employers—whether law firms, solo practitioners, or corporations—probably recruit heavily from the local schools. Many students also work part-time as law clerks or interns/externs with various employers during their second and third years. In addition to gaining exposure to the practice of law and developing good skills, working for a local employer could lead to a permanent job upon graduation or enable you to develop contacts useful for obtaining a job upon graduation.

If you live in Louisiana, or in France, Spain, or another civil law country, you may want to consider Tulane, Loyola, L.S.U., or Southern University School of Law, where you can study both a civil and common law curriculum.

Along those same lines, some law schools have faculty or resources renowned in a particular legal specialty, such as international law, environmental law, constitutional law, or entertainment law. If you think you ultimately want to specialize in a specific area, you should investigate which law schools offer the broadest course choices in that area.

If location is not an issue, consider schools that have a national reputation and place their graduates all over the country. But what if you don't think you have the grades or the money to consider one of those schools?

Then you need to think about which law schools can best assure you of two things: passing the Bar and getting a job.

Let's talk about the Bar first. To be a practicing attorney, you have to pass a bar examination. The Bar is a two- or three- day examination given by each state. It tests roughly everything you've learned over the three years of law school and often many subjects you may not have taken.

One day of the Bar is the multi-state examination, a multiple-choice test used in every state except Louisiana. The remaining one or two days consists of essays that test the specific law of the state where you're taking the Bar. Each state has a different bar passage rate. While the Bar is difficult no matter where you take it, certain states (like California and New York) have a particularly low passage rate. For more information go online to www.ncbex.org. This site has all the information you need to get started.

So you can probably see now why it's important to investigate the Bar passage rate of the graduates of any law school you're considering. If the law school has a particularly low Bar passage rate among its graduates, you may want to consider other schools because *if you can't pass the Bar, you can't practice law.*

Another important issue to investigate is the law school's rate of success in placing its students in permanent positions upon graduation. The admissions and placement or career services offices usually have this information available.

It's also important to find out whether recruiters from law firms, corporations, or the government actively recruit at the school or whether graduates find jobs by contacting employers on their own. Most schools have extensive programs that include workshops on all aspects of the job search process, individual counseling, and fall and spring on-campus recruiting programs where employers interview students on campus.

It's very important to have a good idea of job prospects for graduates of a particular law school before you spend three years, and probably a lot of money, studying law at a school where only a negligible percentage of their graduates end up employed as lawyers after graduating.

Once you're convinced you've selected a group of law schools where the majority of graduates pass the Bar and get a job after graduation, you may want to consider factors that affect your experience while in law school. We're talking about such things as class size, student body diversity, and the existence of a forced curve.

If you perform better in smaller classes and enjoy a more intimate learning experience, you will probably not want to select a law school where the average class size is over one hundred. In addition, if you plan to be a full-time student possibly living on or near the campus, the diversity of the student body may be important in ensuring a pleasant social as well as academic experience.

Some law schools have a forced curve where the bottom five or ten percent of the class has to fail. If you don't work well under this type of pressure, you may not want to consider such a school.

Finally, certain colleges host "law fairs" where representatives from a number of law schools come and provide information on their schools to prospective law students. Because you'll have an opportunity to talk to representatives from a variety of law schools at the same time, law fairs can be a useful way to select potential schools.

Usually, your school's pre-law advisor will know if your school hosts a law fair, and if not, which schools in your area do. Even if you don't end up applying to any of the schools represented at the law fair, it is still a good way to obtain additional information about law school in general.

3 | FINANCIAL ASSISTANCE

Unlike college, there is not a wide selection of grants available for law school programs. Should you need financial assistance, we suggest you contact the law school of your choice to see if fellowships, grants, or work-study programs are available. In many instances, private funding sources are available for students who fit certain specific criteria.

In addition, if you are currently employed, we suggest you check with your employer to see if there is a program that will underwrite its employees' continuing education.

The Federal Stafford Loan program is also available to law students. The Stafford Loan program provides low interest loans to students attending school on at least a half-time basis. For more information on financial aid and in particular, The Stafford Loan Program, contact:

The U.S. Department of Education
Federal Student Aid Info Center
Telephone: (800) 4-FED-AID
Website: fafsa.ed.gov

For more information on financial aid, contact:

The Law School Admission Council
662 Penn Street
Newtown, PA 18940
Telephone: (215) 968-1001
Website: www.lsac.org/jd/finance/financial-aid-overview.asp

Finally, if you think you'll need financial aid while in law school, you may want to include a separate letter to the director of financial aid as part of your law school application. That way, if there are programs available at the schools where you apply, the admissions committee can forward your name to the financial aid office immediately. Since many law school financial aid offices see hundreds of applications every year, visiting the office and talking directly to someone there may distinguish your application.

4 | THE LAW SCHOOL EXPERIENCE

Many books have been written about the law school experience. Some, such as *The Paper Chase*, became motion pictures. Perhaps this is because law school is one of the most intense and challenging academic experiences that one can have.

We won't attempt to go into detail on the psychological aspects of the law school experience. This, of course, will vary with the individual. Rather, we'll concentrate on what to expect in terms of courses and academic workload for each of the three years of law school.

First Year

Most schools require first-year law students to take basic year-long courses. These generally consist of torts, contracts, civil procedure, criminal law, and property, and sometimes constitutional law. Schools may also offer one or two electives during the second semester.

Torts is the study of civil wrongs, such as personal injury cases. Contracts, as the name suggests, is the study of the theory and rules behind contractual relations. Civil procedure is the study of the theory and mechanics of the legal process and the court system.

A criminal law course is divided into two parts: criminal law, the study of the crimes against the individual and property, and criminal procedure, the study of the theory and practice of the prosecution of those crimes. For instance, upon arrest, the rules of criminal procedure require the arresting officer to read the suspect his or her rights. This rule is required to ensure that suspects exercise their rights knowingly.

Property is the study of the legal issues involved in the sale, ownership, and other transfers of interest in real property (land).

In most law schools, one exam at the end of the year determines the grades for the basic first-year courses. Some professors may give a practice exam during the course; however, this typically doesn't count toward the final grade. Generally a large volume of reading is required for each course, sometimes several hundred pages a night *per course.* The assignments are usually actual cases from that course area.

In reading the cases, you are expected to do more than simply memorize the facts. The key is to understand the legal principles illustrated by the case and then be able to apply those principles to other cases. Read the "Study Tips" section of this book for some hints on how to best approach the law school workload.

Once in class, professors often use the Socratic Method. Under this method, professors don't lecture as in college courses. Instead, they call on students randomly and ask the students to explain the court's decision in a particular case. The professor may then give a hypothetical case and ask that same student or another student to explain to the class how the court should rule in light of the court's decision in the case just discussed. Students must be able to reason logically and think quickly on their feet. Section 8 of this book, "Thinking Like a Lawyer: Applying Case Precedent," features an exercise of this type for you to try.

The Socratic Method intimidates some people. The key, however, is to understand the legal principles behind what you are studying and then apply those principles logically to varying fact patterns.

Another first-year event at some schools is the opportunity to participate in a moot court competition. In moot court, students engage in a mock trial. During these competitions, a student can get a feel for what it's like to argue a case before a judge. Although some law schools may not require participation in a first-year moot court competition, we highly recommend it, as moot court is a useful introduction to writing and advocacy skills.

Although difficult to obtain, we highly recommend that you try to secure a summer clerkship after your first year. Clerkships are usually available with law firms, government agencies, judges, and corporations. The best time to apply is after the first semester of your first year, with the application process generally handled through the school's career services office. Clerkships are awarded principally based on your first semester grades. Some employers may consider your entire first year. By the end of the year, many first semester applicants have secured clerkships; therefore, it is critical that you apply early for these positions.

Second Year

Second-year courses generally aren't any easier than first-year courses. Second year, however, may seem a little easier because most people are more confident and the courses run for the semester rather than for the year.

During the second year, it's a good idea to take courses that will be on the Bar Exam. Some of these include evidence, constitutional law, secured transactions, and business entities. It's also advisable to take tax and securities regulation if you're interested in corporate or business law.

Second year is also the time to take courses in specialized areas, such as international law, copyright law, or entertainment law.

In the beginning of the second year, most schools determine whether you will make law review. Law review members are the top students in their class based on grades or, in some cases, based on a writing competition. The law review publishes the highest scholarly journal for the school. Law review members edit the articles submitted by professors and practitioners, as well as pieces submitted by fellow law review members.

In addition to the law review, some schools have legal journals that give students the opportunity to write and edit articles on specialized areas of the law, such as environmental law, civil rights law, or international law. For anyone seeking a career in academia, some type of law review or journal experience is essential.

During the second year, a good deal of time is also devoted to finding a summer legal internship, usually with a law firm or government agency. Often, prospective employers will visit schools during the fall to interview second-and third-year students for both permanent and summer jobs.

It's important to try to get a legal job following your second year because if you do well in that job, you may get an offer for permanent employment following graduation. If employers don't come to your law school to recruit, it's still important to contact them yourself since a job during your second-year summer is also an important introduction to what the practice of law is like.

Third Year

Third-year courses are similar to second-year courses. During third year, however, most students are even more relaxed than second year and thus better able to deal with the continuing academic pressures.

Major issues of the third year are getting a job after graduation and passing the Bar. If you've been lucky enough to get an offer for permanent employment following your second-year summer job, that's one less thing to worry about. If not, third year is the time to really begin contacting prospective employers and setting up interviews.

As discussed earlier, passing the Bar is required to practice law. Bar review courses usually start in May or June. There is, however, a legal ethics part to the Bar usually taken during your third year.

Finally, some students decide to pursue a Masters in Law (an LLM). This is generally a one-year program following third year. An LLM allows a student to specialize in a particular area of the law, such as taxation or international relations. People may decide to pursue an LLM for a number of reasons. These may include going into academia (although an LLM is not required) or developing expertise in a complicated area of the law such as corporate taxation.

Clinical Programs

Many law schools offer clinical programs during the second and third years of law school. Clinical programs offer law students hands-on experience counseling clients and, in certain programs, appearing in court or administrative proceedings on behalf of indigent clients.

In certain trial clinical programs, a law student will specialize in a specific area such as criminal law cases, civil cases, or juvenile court cases. Then, under the supervision of a practicing attorney or a law professor, the student will represent an indigent client. Representation will usually include all aspects of the attorney/client relationship from counseling the client to representing him or her in court.

Some prison legal assistance programs also give law students the opportunity to represent incarcerated clients under the supervision of a practicing attorney or law professor. Oftentimes, the representation of these clients will include aiding the prisoner in drafting *writs of habeas corpus* when the prisoner feels that he or she has been unjustly imprisoned. Law students may also aid prisoners in drafting appeals for their cases or advocating better living conditions.

Regardless of the type of law you ultimately choose to practice, clinical programs are an excellent way to begin a commitment to helping the less fortunate in your community while simultaneously developing practical legal skills.

Study Tips (by Paul Weisenfeld, Esq.)

College students interested in attending law school are surely aware that effective study habits are very personal. What works for one individual will not necessarily work for another. Some people feel most comfortable spending their time in the library, while others study in solitude in their room. Still others spend their study time engaging their fellow students in intellectual discourse. Some formalize this process by joining study groups, a popular and effective option. Despite the competitive nature of law school, your decision about how to spend your study time should be dictated not by what others do, but by what makes you most comfortable with the material and by what you've found has worked from your past experience.

Deciding what to focus on when reading the materials is more important than how much time to spend studying and where to do it. There are many different aspects to a law school education and to being a lawyer. The law itself is only one of them. As a professor told my first-year law school class: You're not here to learn or memorize the law—you can always look that up. Thus, when reading and thinking about the case materials, rather than focusing exclusively on the law (i.e., the holding or outcome of a particular case), you should focus on (a) why the given facts, as applied to the law, compel a particular holding; (b) how altering pieces of the fact pattern or presenting the facts in different ways will lead to different holdings and why that's true; and (c) how such changes in the fact pattern allow you to construct different arguments to represent the interests of one side or the other. Focusing on these aspects rather than solely on the holdings will help prepare you for the varied roles that lawyers play in society. The more prominent roles today include lawyer as legislator, advocate, and judge. Lawyers can be concerned with promoting certain public policy goals through legislation, advancing the interests of a particular client, or by applying the intent of lawmakers to the facts of the case before them.

Notwithstanding my first-year professor's remark and my comments up to this point, you will, nonetheless, have to memorize a substantial amount of law to get through law school exams and the Bar Exam. To do this, it's important to break down legal doctrines into their constitutive elements. In the area of criminal law, as this book demonstrates, you must prove all of a crime's necessary elements to establish the crime. This basic principle is equally applicable to other areas of the law. In the context of litigation, for instance, a plaintiff must prove all of the elements of his claim to prevail, whether he brings a claim on due process grounds, principles of tort law, property rights, or contract. Similarly, when constructing, analyzing, or memorizing defenses to claims, be aware of all the necessary elements. The key to successful exams is to be methodical in your analysis of each element. You must subject each possible claim and defense to thorough scrutiny by offering arguments in favor of and against the establishment of each of their elements.

In addition, one study technique worthy of note is that of briefing your case. All too often first-year students begin the year by briefing cases (outlining the facts, holding, and rules of law, as we'll show you in the next section) only to become complacent by mid-semester. They end up doing only terse summaries, at best, believing that thoroughly briefing the case is no longer necessary. One word of caution:

Do not fall into this trap. Briefing cases throughout the first year is a thoroughly worthwhile endeavor. Not only does briefing cases teach you the discipline of analyzing each important aspect of a particular case, but it also teaches the student to differentiate between important matters and less relevant facts in a timely and efficient manner. This skill will be invaluable during exams when you have a limited amount of time and usually must sift through extensive fact patterns. Furthermore, the discipline of briefing cases helps during the Bar Exam when you need to analyze a case quickly and correctly and then decide which response is most appropriate. Briefing cases also helps you to prepare essential course outlines when you are studying for exams at the end of the semester. You will have already neatly outlined your case briefs. Do not underestimate the importance of this exercise which, at first, may appear to be sheer drudgery. It is very important and can only help you to master the practice of law. Preparing such course outlines is perhaps the most effective way of understanding the course material as a whole. Organizing each course into an outline will allow you to grasp the interconnections between seemingly disparate cases.

By far one of the most important study tips to offer anyone going to law school is to be well-organized and disciplined. Read your assignments on a daily basis because the volume of work will be considerable and one can quickly find oneself trying to play catch up. You will cover far too much material to try and cram at the end of the semester. The course loads are extremely heavy and you put yourself under too much pressure. Do the assignments as they are given and you will have no trouble keeping up. Pacing yourself at the outset and being an effective manager of your time is essential and a critical lifeskill to master. Above all, do not get caught up in the competitive milieu of law school. Remember that if you spend too much time worrying about what other students are doing, you have that much less time to spend on your own work.

5 | EMPLOYMENT OPPORTUNITIES AFTER LAW SCHOOL

A law school education develops analytical and problem-solving skills prized by a wide variety of employers. This may explain why lawyers are found everywhere from the traditional practice of law to running Fortune 500 corporations. We'll discuss below some of the many legal and non-legal options available to a law school graduate.

Legal Options

Many law school graduates follow the traditional route after law school. This usually involves working at a law firm or a government agency. Some graduates also open up a private practice.

Law firms vary in size, practice specialty, and work atmosphere. Large "white shoe" firms, with anywhere from fifty to several hundred attorneys, generally recruit from the top law schools and represent Fortune 500 corporate clients and high net worth individuals. These firms are usually divided into departments such as corporate, litigation, trusts and estates, tax, and real estate.

In Washington D.C., many of the firms do work related to the federal government. Others do legal work related to lobbying or have additional practice specialties such as environmental law and administrative litigation.

In some firms, first year associates do a "rotation" through several departments before deciding on a specialty area. In other firms, a practice area is assigned to entering associates and they work in that area their entire time at that firm.

The organization of the firm and the ratio between partners (i.e., owners of the firm) and associates (employees) determines whether first year associates will work with either one partner, a group of partners or, in some cases, work almost exclusively with senior or mid-level associates.

Associates usually receive performance reviews at least once a year and often raises are tied to the review. In addition, a firm may ask an associate to leave if he or she does not pass the Bar (although generally an associate has two attempts to pass the Bar before they're asked to leave).

Generally, the larger and more prestigious law firms have plush offices, closely resembling the offices of their corporate clients. Services such as word processing, copying, proofreading, and messenger services usually operate twenty-four hours a day. In addition, when clients come to the offices for meetings, neighboring restaurants often provide lavish catering.

While this may all sound glamorous, the flip side is that attorneys, primarily associates, are also expected to be available twenty-four hours a day. It is not unusual to pull "all nighters" at the firm when working on a major corporate deal or a brief.

Associates are expected to work extremely hard (since generally you are also being paid very high salaries) and cancel personal plans as often as necessary. In addition, all attorneys at the firm (including partners) must fill out daily time sheets, recording all work activities down to the quarter of an hour. Associates need to generate a certain minimum number of "billable" hours per year, generally 1,800 to 2,000 hours. A forty-hour workweek is usually not acceptable at most major firms.

The road to partnership, i.e. when you become an owner of the firm (although some firms are now professional corporations), lasts anywhere from seven to nine years, depending on the firm. If partnership is something you are aiming for, you can expect to work extremely hard with no guarantee that at the end of the seven-to-nine year period you'll get that "brass ring," or partnership.

In addition to judging the quality of your work and your lawyering skills, many firms judge prospective partners on their ability to bring business to the firm. Associates are considered for partnership with their entering class, although depending upon the economic prosperity of the firm, there may be some years when no one in a particular class will make partner.

There are other options in private law practice besides working at a large firm. Small and mid-sized firms often offer the same degree of challenging legal work and many times in a more relaxed atmosphere. However, the salaries may not be as high, and although there may be a more congenial atmosphere, associates still work very hard.

Small firms are also more subject to economic changes and recessionary downturns than larger firms are, particularly if one or two clients generate most of their business, or by one or two "rainmakers," or partners who generate a lot of business. If one of these major clients or rainmaker partners leaves the firm, the firm may lay off attorneys. Generally, associates and "non-productive" partners—partners who don't generate business for the firm—are the first to go.

Opportunities are also available clerking for a judge, either at the state or federal level, for one or two years. Generally federal clerkships—either with a district court judge, a judge on the U.S.

Court of Appeals, and ultimately with the U.S. Supreme Court—are the most competitive and prestigious clerkships.

Although clerkships usually pay less than a position in a law firm, these positions are highly sought after for a number of reasons.

First, if you're considering a career in academia or in a policymaking government job, a clerkship is often an unwritten prerequisite.

In addition, if you're considering litigation, a clerkship on either the state or federal level provides invaluable exposure to the court system. The clerkship is essentially an apprenticeship where you work closely with a judge. Judges usually have anywhere from one to three clerks.

Each judge runs his or her chambers differently. Some clerks are an integral part of the decision-making process, including writing bench memoranda and drafting opinions. In other chambers, clerks are limited to doing legal research for opinions that the judge will write. Most federal court clerkships are obtained by writing judges the fall semester of the second year of law school. Typically these judges select their clerks a year in advance. During the fall semester of the third year, students write judges for clerkships with state courts and specialty courts such as bankruptcy, tax, and the U.S. Court of Federal Claims. A recommendation from one or more professors is helpful and often an unwritten requirement for obtaining one of the more prestigious federal clerkships.

Another traditional legal option for a law school graduate is to work on the in-house legal staff of a corporation. Generally, however, corporations don't hire directly from law school for these positions, since they usually prefer lawyers with at least two to three years of experience.

The U.S. Attorney's office, a highly sought after litigation opportunity, requires several years of litigation experience before hiring. For graduates interested in criminal law, the offices of the local district attorney usually hires graduates directly from law school.

In addition, practicing with the Legal Aid Society provides attorneys with a broad exposure to various areas of civil law, including landlord/tenant and family law.

In the area of international law, opportunities include the Legal Advisors office of the State Department and the Office of the General Counsel at the Agency for International Development, the Overseas Private Investment Corporation, the Export Import Bank, and the Trade and Development Agency. The World Bank, the International Monetary Fund, the regional development banks, and the United Nations also have legal divisions that handle a wide variety of international issues. In Paris, France, UNESCO (United Nations, Educational, Scientific, and Cultural Organization) has a legal division. Like the in-house corporate positions, jobs with the international organizations and the State Department require two to three years of experience after law school.

If international law is an area that interests you, you should take some international law courses and contact any of the above organizations while in law school to explore summer positions available for second-year law students. This would provide you with an introduction to the work and the people making the hiring decisions.

Entertainment law is another area of increasing interest. There are four major areas of entertainment law—music, film, television, and sports law. Most of the major studios (Sony Pictures, Fox, Paramount, Universal, and Warner Brothers) have in-house legal divisions, as do the networks and cable companies such as HBO, Showtime, Lifetime, and Turner Broadcasting.

On the music side of entertainment, there are legal jobs with the major recording companies such as MCA, Sony, and Motown Records. Law firms specializing in entertainment are located primarily in New York and Los Angeles.

Sports law can be an exciting area. The networks have lawyers who specialize in sports work. In addition, some of the larger sports management companies, such as International Management Group and ProServ, may hire in-house lawyers. The NFL, Major League Baseball, and the NBA also have in-house legal staffs.

Because entertainment law is an extremely competitive field, two to three years of experience as a general corporate lawyer is usually required. Oftentimes, particularly in the music area, some direct entertainment experience on the non-legal side may also be desirable.

Academia is a challenging area for graduates who find studying, researching, writing, and teaching law interesting. Some law schools hire directly after law school for junior faculty positions. Most law schools search for candidates with top grades, law review experience, judicial clerkship experience, and an LLM (a Masters in law in a specific area). In addition, experience in the actual practice of law is a plus. To increase your chances of obtaining one of these positions, it is advisable to try to publish an article on a legal issue while in law school. Strong recommendations from law school professors are also helpful if you're interested in legal academia.

If you are a member of your law school's law review, publishing an article or shorter piece is required. If you are not a member of a law review, you can still have the opportunity to publish by completing a scholarly legal paper and sending it to a legal journal at your school or another law school's law review. Most law reviews accept articles from law students from other schools. Since so much of academic work involves writing and research, it's important to demonstrate that you have those abilities before you actually apply for the job.

Local, state, and federal government agencies also have legal positions available directly after law school. On the local level, the city attorney's office handles all legal matters for the city. Often, local city councils and county boards hire lawyers for their staffs. On the state level, state agencies, such as transit authorities, public utilities, and legislative counsels for state legislatures, have legal positions available.

On the national level, most of the U.S. government agencies, such as the Department of Health and Human Services, the Department of Education, the Department of Energy, the Department of Housing and Urban Development, the FBI, the CIA, the Department of Transportation, the Department of Agriculture, the Department of the Treasury, and the Department of Justice, all have sizeable legal staffs. These agencies are located primarily in Washington, D.C. and most hire directly after law school.

If working on Capital Hill interests you, all of the congressional and senatorial committees, as well as the personal staffs of the elected officials, have legal positions. Some of these positions are available directly after law school, but generally, some type of legal experience is required. Members of Congress often hire lawyers for non-legal staff positions.

In the area of fine arts and culture, the Smithsonian Institute has in-house lawyers, as do most of the major museums such as the Metropolitan Museum in New York. Again, however, these positions usually require several years of general corporate legal experience.

Public interest law is an additional area that offers challenging work and often a high degree of job satisfaction, particularly when you represent individuals or groups that may not otherwise be able to afford legal counsel.

The Anti-Defamation League, the American Civil Liberties Union, the NAACP Legal Defense Fund, the Lawyers Committee for Civil Rights under Law, the Mexican American Legal Defense and Educational Fund, and the Children's Defense Fund are a few of the many public interest positions available to young lawyers. Like all areas of the law, public interest work is intellectually rigorous and demanding. However, despite lower pay than what is available in most firms, many attorneys choose public interest law because of the relatively greater opportunities to interact with their clients and to be a part of social and economic change.

Generally positions in the larger law firms offer the highest paying positions, with some in-house corporate positions (including entertainment and international law positions) paying competitive salaries. As mentioned, work in a district attorney's office, a public defenders office, and the U.S. Attorney's office will usually pay considerably less. Ultimately, however, there are other lifestyle trade-offs and job satisfaction issues that should be seriously considered before deciding which area best suits you.

Non-legal Options

Increasingly, law school graduates are deciding to pursue non-legal work. Because many employers view the law school training as a valuable asset, many opportunities for lawyers who decide not to practice law exist. For this reason, lawyers can be found as college presidents, diplomats, cabinet members, Senators, congressional representatives, studio heads, screenwriters, agents, and in just about any field with the exception of those where specialized training, such as medicine or science, is needed.

The key to obtaining a non-legal position is to decide which area interests you and then demonstrate to a prospective employer that you can use your legal training effectively to do the job you're seeking.

If you ultimately decide that practicing law is not for you, it's worth persevering until you get the non-legal job you really want. Because once you accept a legal job, you can be pretty much guaranteed of working long hours—with little, if any time—to look for another job.

6 | THE ANATOMY OF A CASE: A CASE BRIEFING EXERCISE

The Anatomy of a Case

As mentioned in the "Study Tips" section, briefing a case is an important and necessary task. Simply put, it is the dissection of a legal decision into a short form. This process is important because it forces you to look at the guts of a legal decision and reduce the same to an easily accessible bite of information. The key elements of a legal decision are:

1. The facts (the circumstances that give rise to the question before the court).

2. The issue (or the question before the court).

3. The proceeding below (if it's a higher court ruling, the lower court's decision is usually noted). If you are reading a lower court case, these will be the first proceedings and hence there are no proceedings below.

4. The holding (the legal conclusions reached by the court). In a Court

of Appeals case, the court will remand the case back to the lower court, affirm the lower court's ruling, or overrule it.

5. The reason for the court's decision (the court's analysis of holding).

Later in this book is a sample case, read it carefully. Then read it again. During your second read, highlight the elements of the case according to the outline provided above. For instance, after you've identified the facts, make a notation in the margin ("facts"). Do the same for the other elements of the case.

The People of Michigan v. Graham Donit

Graham Donit shot Robert Blair while stealing his car. Robert died and Graham was charged with the crime of murder. Graham claimed that he wasn't read his rights, he was denied counsel, and was coerced to confess to the murder. As a result, Graham asked the court to dismiss the charge of murder against him because his rights were violated.

The prosecution had presented evidence showing that when the defendant was arrested, he had flippantly recited his rights to the arresting officer before the officer could read him his rights.

The prosecution argued that the defendant had waived the right to have his rights read by reciting them himself. The district court (the lower court) ruled that unless the defendant clearly and unequivocally states that he doesn't want his rights read, the arresting officer is bound to read the defendant his rights at the time of arrest. The district court dismissed the charges against the defendant. The prosecution appealed to the Court of Appeals claiming that Graham had voluntarily waived his rights.

The Court of Appeals overruled the district court's decision and held that the defendant had indeed waived his rights. The court reasoned that the defendant's flippant recitation of his rights was a sufficient action to constitute a waiver and thus the arresting officer was not bound to read the defendant his rights.

Model Brief

The People of Michigan v. Graham Donit

Facts:
The defendant was arrested and charged with first-degree murder. The arresting officer did not read the defendant his rights because, upon the defendant's arrest, he flippantly recited his rights before the arresting officer could read them to him.

Issue:
The relevant issue on appeal is whether defendant's due process rights were violated by the officer's failure to read him his rights at the time of arrest.

Proceedings Below:
The district court held that defendant's due process rights had been violated by the arresting officer's failure to read him his rights at the time of defendant's arrest.

Holding:
The Court of Appeals overruled the lower court.

Reasons for the Decision:
The Court of Appeals reasoned that, although the arresting officer didn't read the defendant his rights, the defendant's flippant recitation of his rights to the police officer was sufficient proof that the defendant understood his rights and, therefore, his due process rights were not violated.

The key to briefing a case properly is to get to the essence of the case and to clearly understand the legal issue or issues that are before the court. For example, in the set of facts set forth above, there may be facts in evidence about the shooting, as well as the facts that gave rise to the claim that Graham wasn't read his rights.

Thus, there are potentially two legal issues before the court— the first is whether the defendant is guilty of first-degree murder. The second issue is whether the arresting officer properly read the defendant his rights.

In our example, however, the court is *only* addressing the issue of whether the defendant was properly read his rights. Whether the defendant is actually guilty of murder is not before the court and therefore should not be included as an issue when briefing the case.

Once you understand the issues before the court, it's easier to understand the court's holding and the reasons for its decision. And once you understand why a particular set of facts would give rise to a specific holding, you're on your way to being able to understand how an analogous, although completely different set of facts, could either give rise to a similar holding or be distinguished. Take, for example, a case in which a judge holds that although the facts may seem to be analogous, enough key differences exist that give rise to a different holding.

This is what lawyers mean when they refer to case "precedent" Now that you understand the basics of briefing a case, let's move on to some actual cases.

Instructions: Case Briefing Exercise

The following five cases are from each of the basic first-year courses: civil procedure, contracts, property, torts, and constitutional law. These cases have been adjudicated by various courts. Carefully read each case and then brief the case using the previously discussed format. There are sample case briefs following the cases so you can check your mastery of case briefing skills.

The purpose of this exercise is to give you a jump on a major part of the law school experience—briefing cases—and to give you another opportunity to determine whether you have the interest and the affinity to do the type of work expected of law students and lawyers.

Take as much time as you need and good luck!

Civil Procedure

CALDER
v.
JONES

REINQUIST, J., delivered the opinion for a unanimous Court.

John G. Kester argued the cause for petitioners. With him on the briefs was *Aubrey M. Daniel III.*
Paul S. Ablon argued the cause for respondent. With him on the brief were *Stephen S. Monroe* and *Richard P Towne.*

JUSTICE REINQUIST delivered the opinion of the Court.

Respondent Shirley Jones brought suit in California Superior Court claiming that she had been libeled in an article written and edited by petitioners in Florida. The article was published in a national magazine with a large circulation in California. Petitioners were served with process by mail in Florida and caused special appearances to be entered on their behalf, moving to quash the service of process for lack of personal jurisdiction. The Superior Court granted the motion on the ground that First Amendment concerns weighed against an assertion of jurisdiction otherwise proper under the Due

Process Clause. The California Court of Appeal reversed, rejecting the suggestion that First Amendment considerations enter into the jurisdictional analysis. We now affirm.

Respondent lives and works in California. She and her husband brought this suit against the *National Enquirer, Inc.,* its local distributing company, and petitioners for libel, invasion of privacy, and intentional infliction of emotional harm. The *National Enquirer* is a Florida corporation with its principal place of business in Florida. It publishes a national weekly newspaper with a total circulation of more than 5 million. About 600,000 of those copies, almost twice the level of the next highest state, are sold in California. Respondent's and her husband's claims were based on an article that appeared in the *National Enquirer*'s October 9, 1979 issue. Both the National Enquirer and the distributing company answered the complaint and made no objection to the jurisdiction of the California court.

Petitioner South is a reporter employed by the *National Enquirer.* He is a resident of Florida, though he frequently travels to California on business. South wrote the first draft of the challenged article, and his byline appeared on it. He did most of his research in Florida, relying on phone calls to sources in California for the information contained in the article. Shortly before publication, South called respondent's home and read a draft of the article to her husband to elicit his comments upon it. Aside from his frequent trips and phone calls, South has no other relevant contacts with California.

Petitioner Calder is also a Florida resident. He has been to California only twice—once on a pleasure trip prior to the publication of the article and once after to testify in an unrelated trial. Calder is president and editor of the *National Enquirer.* He "oversee[s] just about every function of the *(National) Enquirer.*" App. 24. He reviewed and approved the initial evaluation of the subject of the article and edited it in its final form. He also declined to print a retraction requested by respondent. Calder has no other relevant contacts with California.

In considering petitioners' motion to quash service of process, the Superior Court surmised that the actions of petitioners in Florida, causing injury to respondent in California, would ordinarily be sufficient to support an assertion of jurisdiction over them in California. But the court felt that special solicitude was necessary because of the potential "chilling effect" on reporters and editors, which would result from requiring them to appear in remote jurisdictions to answer for the content of articles upon which they worked. The court also noted that respondent's rights could be "fully satisfied" in her suit against the publisher without requiring petitioners to appear as parties. The Superior Court, therefore, granted the motion.

The California Court of Appeal reversed. 138 Cal. App. 3d 128, 187 Cal. Rptr. 825 (1982). The court agreed that neither petitioners contacts with California would be sufficient for an assertion of jurisdiction on a cause of action unrelated to those contacts. See *Perkins v. Benguet Mining Co.*, 342 U. S. 437 (1952) (permitting general jurisdiction where defendant's contacts with the forum were "continuous and systematic"). But the court concluded that a valid basis for jurisdiction existed on the theory that petitioners intended to, and did, cause tortious injury to respondent in California. The fact that the actions causing the effects in California were performed outside the state did not prevent the state from asserting jurisdiction over a cause of action arising out of those effects. The court rejected the Superior Court's conclusion that First Amendment considerations must be weighed in the scale against jurisdiction.

The Supreme Court of California denied a timely petition for hearing. App. 122. On petitioners' appeal to this Court, probable jurisdiction was postponed. 460 U. S. 1080 (1983). We conclude that jurisdiction by appeal does not lie. *Kulko v. California Superior Court,* 436 U. S. 84, 90, and n. 4 (1978). Treating the jurisdictional statement as a petition for *writ of certiorari,* as we are authorized to do, 28 U. S. C. §2103, we hereby grant the petition.

The Due Process Clause of the Fourteenth Amendment to the United States Constitution permits personal jurisdiction over a defendant in any state with which the defendant has "certain minimum contacts . . . such that the maintenance of the suit does not offend 'traditional notions of fair play and substantial justice.'" *Milliken v. Meyer,* 311 U. S. 457, 463" *International Shoe Co. v. Washington,* 326 U. S. 310, 316 (1945). In judging minimum contacts, a court properly focuses on "the relationship among the defendant, the forum, and the litigation" *Shaffer v. Heitner,* 433 U. S. 186, 204 (1977). See also *Rush v. Savchuk,* 444 U. S. 320, 332 (1980). The plaintiff's lack of "contacts" will not defeat otherwise proper jurisdiction, see *Keeton v. HustlerMagazine, Inc.,* ante, at 779-781, but they may be so manifold as to permit jurisdiction when it would not exist in their absence. Here, the plaintiff is the focus of the activities of the defendants out of which the suit arises. See *McGee v. International Life Ins. Co.,* 355 U. S. 220 (1957).

The allegedly libelous story concerned the California activities of a California resident. It impugned the professionalism of an entertainer whose television career was centered in California. The article was drawn from California sources, and the brunt of the harm, in terms both of respondent's emotional distress and the injury to her professional reputation, was suffered in California. In sum, California is the focal point both of the story and of the harm suffered. Jurisdiction over petitioners is therefore proper in California based on the "effects" of their Florida conduct in California. *World-Wide Volkswagen Corp. v. Woodson,* 444 U. S. 286, 297-298 (1980); Restatement (Second) of Conflict of Laws §37 (1971).

Petitioners argue that they are not responsible for the circulation of the article in California. A reporter and an editor, they claim, have no direct economic stake in their employers sales in a distant state. Nor are ordinary employees able to control their marketing activity. The mere fact that they can "foresee" that the article will be circulated and have an effect in California is not sufficient for an assertion of jurisdiction. *World-Wide Volkswagen Corp. v. Woodson, supra,* at 295; *Rush v. Savchuk, supra,* at 328-329. They do not "in effect appoint the [article their] agent for service of process." *World-Wide Volkswagen Corp. v. Woodson, supra,* at 296. Petitioners liken themselves to a welder employed in Florida who works on a boiler that subsequently explodes in California. Cases that hold that jurisdiction will be proper over the manufacturer, *Buckeye Boiler Co. v. Superior Court,* 71 Cal. 2d 893, 458 P. 2d 57 (1969); *Gray v. American Radiator & Standard Sanitary Corp.,* 22 Ill. 2d 432, 176 N. E. 2d 761 (1961), should not be applied to the welder who has no control over and derives no direct benefit from his employer's sales in that distant state.

Petitioners' analogy does not wash. Whatever the status of their hypothetical welder, petitioners are not charged with mere untargeted negligence. Rather, their intentional, and allegedly tortious, actions were expressly aimed at California. Petitioner South wrote and petitioner Calder edited an article that they knew would have a potentially devastating impact upon respondent. They knew that the brunt of that injury would be felt by respondent in the state in which she lives and works and in which the National Enquirer has its largest circulation. Under the circumstances, petitioners must "reasonably anticipate being haled into court there" to answer for the truth of the statements made in their article. *World-Wide Volkswagen Corp. v. Woodson, supra,* at 297; Kulko v. California Superior Court, supra, at 97-98; Shaffer v. Heitner, supra, at 216. An individual injured in California need not go to Florida to seek redress from persons who, though remaining in Florida, knowingly cause the injury in California.

Petitioners are correct that their contacts with California are not to be judged according to their employer's activities there. On the other hand, their status as employees does not somehow insulate them from jurisdiction. Each defendant's contacts with the forum state must be assessed individually. See *Rush v. Savchuk, supra,* at 332 ("The requirements of *International Shoe . . .* must be met as to each defendant over whom a state court exercises jurisdiction"). In this case, petitioners are primary participants in an alleged wrongdoing intentionally directed at a California resident and jurisdiction over them is proper on that basis.

We also reject the suggestion that First Amendment concerns enter into the jurisdictional analysis. The infusion of such considerations would needlessly complicate an already imprecise inquiry. *Estin v. Estin,* 334 U. S. 541, 545 (1948). Moreover, the potential chill on protected First Amendment activity stemming from libel and defamation actions is already taken into account in the constitutional limitations on the substantive law governing such suits. See *New York Times Co. v. Sullivan,* 376 U. S. 254 (1964); *Gertz v. Robert Welch, Inc.,* 418 U. S. 323 (1974). To reintroduce those concerns at the jurisdictional stage would be a form of double counting. We have already declined in other contexts to grant special procedural protections to defendants in libel and defamation actions in addition to the constitutional protections embodied in the substantive laws. See, e.g., *Herbert v. Lando,* 441 U. S. 153 (1979) (no First Amendment privilege bars inquiry into editorial process). See also *Hutchinson v. Proxmire,* 443 U. S. 111, 120, n. 9 (1979) (implying that no special rules apply for summary judgment).

We hold that jurisdiction over petitioners in California is proper because of their intentional conduct in Florida calculated to cause injury to respondent in California. The judgment of the California Court of Appeal is *Affirmed.*

Your Brief

_____

_____

_____

_____

_____

_____

_____

_____

_____

_____

_____

_____

_____

_____

_____

_____

_____

_____

_____

_____

_____

_____

_____

_____

_____

_____

_____

_____

_____

Model Brief

Calder v. Jones, 466 U.S. 783

Facts:

Respondent Shirley Jones and her husband sued the *National Enquirer* in California for an allegedly libelous article written by petitioner South, a reporter employed by the *National Enquirer* and edited by petitioner Calder, the editor of the *National Enquirer*. Both Calder and South were Florida residents. The *National Enquirer* has substantial sales in California, and its largest circulation is in California.

Petitioners moved to quash the service of process against them on the grounds of lack of personal jurisdiction.

Issues:

The following issues were presented to the court:

(1) Where defendants do not live in the state seeking jurisdiction over them and have no other "minimum contacts" with the state, is the fact that they can foresee that their actions (in this case writing and approving the article) would have effect in California sufficient to exercise jurisdiction over them; and

(2) In a libel case in which there are otherwise sufficient minimum contacts to exercise personal jurisdiction over a defendant, should First Amendment concerns affect the jurisdictional analysis.

Proceedings Below:

The California Superior Court granted petitioners motion to quash personal service based on First Amendment concerns weighed against granting an otherwise proper exercise of personal jurisdiction. The California Court of Appeals reversed the Superior Court's ruling, holding that the assertion of jurisdiction in California was proper. The Court of Appeals reasoned that the defendants intentionally caused tortious injury in California.

Holding:
The U.S. Supreme Court affirmed the ruling of the California Court of Appeals, holding that the defendants conduct in Florida had sufficient effects in California to justify jurisdiction in California.

Reasons for the Decision:
The court held that jurisdiction over the petitioner was proper in California because their intentional conduct was calculated to cause harm in California. The court concluded that petitioners knew that respondent Jones lived and worked in California, that the *National Enquirer* had its largest circulation in that state, and thus they knew that the "brunt of the injury would be felt" in California. Therefore, they should have reasonably anticipated "being haled into court" to answer for the truth of the statements made in the article.

The court also reasoned that First Amendment concerns should not enter into the jurisdictional analysis since the "potential chill on First Amendment freedoms had already been taken into account in the constitutional limits on substantive law governing those suits." The court further reasoned that to do otherwise would in essence be "double counting."

Property

35 N.Y.2d 634

Arthur R. BRAND, III, as Trustee, et al.,

Respondents,

v.

Richard PRINCE, Appellant.

Court of Appeals of New York.

Dec. 20, 1974.

JASEN, Judge.

The parties own adjoining farmlands in the town of Deposit, Delaware County. A ten-acre parcel of vacant land lying between their properties is the subject of this action to establish title pursuant to article I5 of the Real Property Actions and Proceedings Law.

After a trial without a jury, the County Court adjudged that neither party had established title by deed, that the plaintiff failed to establish title by adverse possession and, implicitly at least, that the defendant was entitled to possession. The Appellate Division unanimously reversed, on the law and the facts, and directed judgment for the plaintiff on the ground that title by adverse possession had been shown. The defendant's appeal is before us as of right. (CPLR 5601, subd. [a].)

Acquisition of title by adverse possession derives historically from the early English statutes limiting actions to recover land. Truly Statutes of Limitation, their purpose was "for quieting of men's estates, and avoiding of suits" (Statute of Limitations, 21 Jac. I, ch. 16). The necessary effect, by barring the real owner's right to recover his property, is, of course, to extinguish his title and make absolute the wrongful possessor's.

[1,2] Actual possession adverse to the true owner for the statutory period is required before title will vest. In qualifying the character of the possession required at common law, it is usually said that it must be hostile and under claim of right, actual, open and notorious, exclusive and continuous. (e. g., *Belotti v. Bickhardt*, 2Z8 N.Y. 296,302, 127 ~.E. 2.W.) Reduced to its essentials, this means nothing more than that there must be possession in fact of a type that would give the owner a cause of action in ejectment against the occupier throughout the prescriptive period. (See, generally, J American Law of Property, § 15.3.) To be sure, there are additional statutory requirements as well, whether the possession is underwritten instrument (Real Property Actions and Proceedings Law, §§ 511, 512) or unless claim of title not written (§§ 521, 522).

[3] In the case before us, we find ample support in the record (or the conclusion reached by the Appellate Division), that the common-law requirements for acquisition of title by adverse possession were satisfied. There was testimony that from about 1945 or 1946 to 1961, the ten-acre parcel had been in continuous farming use under the direction and control of plaintiff's predecessors, in conjunction with their tenancy and then ownership of the adjoining parcel. There was additional testimony that when they purchased the adjoining parcel in 1956, the boundary line, as pointed out, included the disputed ten acres. The testimony of the attorney for the estate from which they purchased tended to confirm this. The plaintiff also accounted for use of the disputed land following his purchase in 1961. He testified that the land was posted and rented to a hunting club and that a part was rented for pasturage and haying. Also, there was evidence of fencing and substantial enclosure in conjunction with all these uses, thus satisfying the statute. (Real Property Actions and Proceedings Law, § 512.) Because the plaintiff was in possession for less than fifteen years,* it was necessary for him to tack his adverse possession to that of his predecessor to satisfy the applicable statutory period. (Former Civ.Prac. Act, § 34.) The question arises as to whether this was proper because the parcel adversely possessed was not within the description of the deed to the plaintiff.

[4,5] The rule is that successive adverse possessions of property omitted from a deed description, especially contiguous property, may be tacked if it appears that the adverse possessor intended to and actually turned over possession of the undescribed part with the portion of the land included in the deed. (*Belotti v. Bickhardt,* 228 N.Y. 296,303, 308, 127 N.E. 23S 241, 243, supra; Adverse Possession-Tacking, Ann., 17 A.L.R.2d 1128, 1131, 1132); (3 American Law of Property, § 15.10.) Because the possessory title is entirely an incident of the adverse holder's possession, transfer of that possession, even

*Plaintiff's deed is dated October 16, 1961.

by parole, means a transfer of the possession by interest. (3 American Law of Property, § 15.10.) The circumstances of this case are entirely consistent with a finding that plaintiff's predecessors intended to and actually turned over their possessory interest in the ten-acre parcel. Hence, the tacking was proper.

Accordingly, the order of the Appellate Division should be affirmed.

BREITEL, C. J., and GABRIELLI, JONES, WACHTLER, SAMUEL RABIN and STEVENS, JJ., concur.

Order affirmed, with costs.

The controversy with respect to title arose some seven years later.

Your Brief

_____

_____

_____

_____

_____

_____

_____

_____

_____

_____

_____

_____

_____

_____

_____

_____

_____

_____

_____

_____

_____

_____

_____

_____

_____

_____

_____

_____

Model Brief

Brand v. Prince, **324 N.E.2d 314**

Facts:
The parties, who own adjoining farmlands, are disputing the title to a ten-acre parcel of land that lies between their properties.

Issues:
The court discussed the following legal issues:

(1) Whether the plaintiff's actions in farming the disputed land were sufficient to establish adverse possession of the land; and

(2) In order to establish the statutory time limit required for adverse possession, could plaintiff "tack" the time that his predecessor adversely possessed the land to the period that the plaintiff adversely possessed such land?

Proceedings Below:
The County Court held that neither party had established title by deed and that the plaintiff had failed to establish adverse possession and thus the defendant was entitled to the property. The Appellate Division unanimously reversed the County Court decision and awarded judgment to the plaintiff because the plaintiff had established adverse possession of the property.

Holding:
The Court of Appeals affirmed the Appellate Division's decision and held that the plaintiff had established title by adverse possession.

Reasons for the Decision:
The Court of Appeals found that, at common law, adverse possession requires that a possessor's actions be hostile under claim of right, actual, open and notorious, exclusive, and continuous. The facts of

this case indicated that the plaintiff rented out part of the land to a hunting club and that a part of the land was rented out for pasturage and haying. The facts also indicated that there was evidence of fencing and substantial enclosure. Thus, the court concluded that the plaintiff's actions had been hostile under claim of right, actual, continuous, open and notorious, and exclusive.

The court also held that plaintiff was entitled to "tack" the period of his predecessor's adverse possession of the land onto his own. The court stated that the rule in such cases was that tacking was allowed to establish the statutory requirement for adverse possession of property omitted from a deed, "especially contiguous property," where it appears that the adverse possessor intended to and actually did turn over possession of the undescribed portion of the land with the portion of the land described in the deed.

In this case, the plaintiff's predecessor had continuously and openly farmed the land before selling it to the plaintiff, and when the plaintiff purchased the land, it was with the belief that it included the disputed ten acres. Thus, the court concluded that the plaintiff's adverse possession of the land had been "continuous" within the meaning of the statute.

Contracts

Ernst LARESE and Barbara Ann Larese, Plaintiffs-Appellants,

v.

CREAMLAND DAIRIES, INC., a New Mexico corporation, Defendant-Appellee.

No. 83-2164.

United States Court of Appeals, *Tenth Circuit.*

July 15, 1985.

Before McKAY and SETH, Circuit Judges and JENKINS, District Judge.

McKAY, Circuit Judge.

The issue in this case is whether a franchisor has an absolute right to refuse to consent to the sale of a franchisee's interest to another prospective franchisee.

Plaintiffs entered into a ten-year franchise agreement with defendant, Creamland Dairies, in 1974. The franchise agreement provided that the franchisee "shall not assign, transfer or sublet this franchise, or any of [the] rights under this agreement, without the prior written consent of Area Franchisor [Creamland] and Baskin Robbins, any such unauthorized assignment, transfer or subletting being null and without effect." The plaintiffs attempted to sell their franchise rights in February and August of 1979, but Creamland refused to consent to the sales. Plaintiffs brought suit, alleging that Creamland had interfered with their contractual relations with the prospective buyers by unreasonably withholding its consent. The District Court granted summary judgment for the defendant because the contract gave the defendant an absolute, unqualified right to refuse to consent to proposed sales of the franchise rights. Plaintiffs appeal, claiming that defendant franchisor has a duty to act in good faith and in a commercially reasonable manner when a franchisee seeks to transfer its rights under the franchise agreement.

The Colorado courts have never addressed the question of whether a franchisor has a duty to act reasonably in deciding whether to consent to a proposed transfer. The Colorado courts have, however, imposed a reasonableness requirement on consent to transfer clauses in other types of contracts. In *Basnett v. Vista Village Mobile Home Park,* 699 P.2d 1343 (Colo. App.1984), the Colorado Appellate

Court held that a landlord cannot unreasonably refuse to consent to assignment or subleasing by a tenant. While the court indicated that the courts would enforce a provision expressly granting the landlord an absolute right to consent if such a provision was freely negotiated, it refused to find such an absolute right in a provision that provided simply that the landlord must consent to Assignment at 1846 *(citing Restatement (2d) of Property § 15.2(2) (1977))*. The question before us, therefore, is whether the Colorado courts would impose a similar requirement of reasonableness on restraint or alienation clauses in franchise agreements.

Counsel for both parties have argued that the franchisor-franchisee relationship is a special one which is not directly analogous to that of a landlord and tenant. All the Supreme Court of Pennsylvania has noted. "[u]nlike a tenant pursuing his own interests while occupying a landlord's property, a franchisee . . . builds the good will of both his own business and [the franchisor]" *Atlantic Richfield v. Razumic,* 480 Pa. 366, 390 A.2d 736, 742 (1978). This aspect of the relationship has led a number of courts to hold that the franchise relationship imposes a duty upon franchisors not to act unreasonably or arbitrarily in terminating the franchise. See, e.g., *Atlantic Richfield,* 390 A.2d at 742; *Arnott v. American Oil Co.,* 609 F.2d 873 (8th Cir.1979), cert. denied, 446 U.S. 918, 100 S.Ct. 1852, 64 L.Ed.2d 272 (1980); *Shell Oil Co. v. Marinello,* 63 N.J. 402, 307 A.2d 598 (1973). As did these courts, we find that the franchisor-franchisee relationship is one that requires the parties to deal with one another in good faith and in a commercially reasonable manner. See *Arnott,* 609 F.2d at 881 (finding fiduciary duty inherent in franchise relationship); *Atlantic Richfield,* 390 A.2d at 742 (basing decision that franchisor cannot arbitrarily terminate relationship on franchisors "obligation to deal with its franchisees in good faith and in a commercially reasonable manner").

Defendants argue that the franchise assignment situation differs from the franchise termination situation in that the franchisor must work with the person to whom the franchise is assigned. To impose a duty of reasonableness, they argue, would violate the rule of United *States v. Colgate & Co.,* 250 U.S. 300. 307. 39 S.Ct. 465, 468, 63 L.Ed. 992 (1919), that a manufacturer engaged in private business has the right "freely to exercise his own independent discretion as to parties with whom he will deal." This right, however, must be balanced against the rights of the franchisees. As is true in the termination cases, the franchisee has invested time and money into the franchise and, in doing so, has created benefits for the franchisor. We do not find it an excessive infringement of the franchisors rights to require that the franchisor act reasonably when the franchisee has decided that it wants out of the relationship. The franchisee should not be forced to choose between losing its investment or remaining in the relationship unwillingly when it has provided a reasonable alternative franchisee.

We do not hold that a provision that expressly grants to the franchisor an absolute right to refuse to consent is unenforceable when such an agreement was freely negotiated. We do not believe the Colorado courts would find such an absolute right, however, in a provision such as the one involved in this case, which provides simply that the franchisee must obtain franchisor consent prior to transfer. See *Vista Village,* at 1346. Rather, the franchisor must bargain for a provision expressly granting the right to withhold consent unreasonably, to ensure that the franchisee is put on notice. Since, in this case, the contracts stated only that consent must be obtained, Creamland did not have the right to withhold consent unreasonably.

Reversed and remanded for further proceedings consistent with this opinion.

Your Brief

_____

_____

_____

_____

_____

_____

_____

_____

_____

_____

_____

_____

_____

_____

_____

_____

_____

_____

_____

_____

_____

_____

_____

_____

_____

_____

_____

_____

_____

_____

Model Brief

Larese v. Creamland Dairies. Inc.

Facts:
Plaintiff entered into a ten-year franchise agreement with defendant, Creamland Dairies. The franchise agreement provided that the franchisee "shall not assign, transfer or sublet this franchise, or any of [the] rights under this agreement, without the prior written consent of Area Franchisor [Creamland] and Baskin Robbins, any such unauthorized assignment, transfer or subletting being null and without effect." The franchisee attempted to sell its franchise rights and the franchisor refused to give its consent.

Issue:
Does a franchisor have an absolute right to refuse consent to the sale of a franchisee's interest to another prospective franchisee?

Proceedings Below:
The district court ruled that the franchisor had an absolute right to refuse to give its consent to a franchisee.

Holding:
The Court of Appeals reversed the district court's ruling and remanded the case for further proceedings consistent with its reasoning.

Reason for Decision:
The Court of Appeals reasoned that the right of a franchisor must be balanced against the right of the franchisee. To require a franchisor to act reasonably toward its franchisee in exercising its right of consent to the sale of a franchise is not an infringement of the franchisor's rights, particularly when the franchisee has been a benefit to the franchisor and the franchisee has provided an alternative

franchisee to the franchisor. If the franchisor wishes to obtain an absolute right to refuse to give consent to a franchisee, the franchisor must bargain separately for such a provision that provides that consent to a transfer can be withheld even *unreasonably*. Absent such a clause, a franchisor cannot withhold consent unreasonably.

Torts

91 Wis.2d 734
James O. PAGELSDORF and Carol L.
Pagelsdorf, Plaintiffs-Appellants,
v.
SAFECO INSURANCE COMPANY OF
AMERICA and Richard J. Mahnke,
Defendants-Respondents.
No. 76-229.
Supreme Court of Wisconsin,
Submitted on Briefs Sept. 12, 1979,
Oct. 9, 1979.

CALLOW, Justice.

[1] We dispose of this appeal by addressing the single issue of the scope of a landlord's duty toward his tenant's invitee who is injured as a result of defective premises. Abrogating the landlord's general cloak of immunity at common law, we hold that a landlord must exercise ordinary care toward his tenant and others on the premises with permission.

The defendant, Richard J. Mahnke, owned a two-story, two-family duplex. There were four balcony porches: one in front and one in back of each flat. Mahnke rented the upper unit to John and Mary Katherine Blattner, who lived there with their three children until Mr. Blattner left the family. Mahnke and his wife lived in the lower unit. The Blattners held the flat under an oral lease that included an agreement that Mahnke would make all necessary repairs on the premises. Mahnke worked as a mechanic for Wisconsin Electric Power Company and considered himself a good handyman.

All the railings on the porches were originally wooden, but Mahnke had begun to replace them with wrought iron as the wooden railings began to deteriorate. By May 10, 1974, wrought iron railings had been placed on the lower back porch, but the wooden railing on the upper back porch had not been replaced. The wooden railing consisted of 2x4s running parallel to the floor of the porch connected by 2x2 spacers running perpendicular to the floor. The railing sections were approximately 3 feet from top to bottom and were between 4 and 6 feet long. They were attached to upright 4x4s by means of nails driven at approximately a 45° angle; none were held in place by screws, bolts, or braces.

Mr. Blattner left the family, and in April 1974, Mrs. Blattner left the apartment and moved with her children to Kansas. She left her furniture in the apartment and paid her rent for the month of May, having arranged with the Mahnkes to have her brothers move the furniture on May 11. On May 10, 1974, Mrs. Blattner's two brothers arrived to move her belongings to Kansas. They rented a truck and parked it behind the duplex. While moving the furniture out of the duplex, they felt they would need help with the heavier items. They asked Carol Pagelsdorf, a next-door neighbor who had been packing Mrs. Blattner's belongings, to ask her husband James to help them. He agreed.

While moving the bedroom furniture, Pagelsdorf and one of Mrs. Blattner's brothers felt that the box spring was too cumbersome to take down the back stairway. The Blattner brother decided the best way to remove it from the apartment would be to lower it from the rear balcony to the ground. Pagelsdorf and a Blattner brother went out on the porch and visually inspected it for safety, but Pagelsdorf did not touch or shake the railings before taking the box spring out. The railings, which had been painted by Mahnke within the past two years, appeared safe. The Blattner brother and Pagelsdorf took the box spring out onto the balcony and leaned it on a railing section. They picked up the spring and leaned over the railing while passing it down to the other brother. While letting the spring down, Pagelsdorf applied pressure straight down on the railing with his body. After both men released the box spring, Pagelsdorf began to straighten up, placing his hands on the railing, and bending his knees slightly. His knees then touched the 2x2 spokes in the railing, and the bottom swung out as if on a hinge. The entire railing section came loose, and Pagelsdorf fell to the ground below, suffering injuries.

Mahnke testified that after the incident, he examined the 4x4 posts and the railing section that gave way and found that the railing ends had dry rot in them. He stated that wood with dry rot would retain its form but not its strength and that this condition would not be readily visible if the wood had been painted over.

Mrs. Blattner testified that Mahnke had warned her of the railing's rotting condition prior to painting the railing. She also testified that several times she had asked Mahnke to repair the railing because it was rotting; she stated that each time, Mahnke responded by telling her that he was busy and would make the repair when he had time to do so. Mahnke testified that prior to the accident he had no knowledge of the rotting condition in the railing and that neither Mrs. Blattner nor her husband ever complained to him about the condition of the railing on the back porch. However, on June 7, 1974, Mahnke gave a statement to an investigator in which he related that several times he had warned Mrs. Blattner to be careful of the upstairs porch railing because he did not trust its strength. Mahnke also testified in a deposition taken April 29, 1976, that he had warned Mrs. Blattner to keep her children off the porch because of his concerns that they would crawl over the railing and that the railing would give way. At trial, Mahnke testified that these warnings merely reflected his distrust of railings in general.

After testimony was closed, the plaintiffs contended that Pagelsdorf's status was that of an invitee of Mahnke and that the jury should be instructed that Mahnke owed him a duty to exercise ordinary care. The plaintiff proposed a special verdict inquiring whether Mahnke was "negligent in failing to keep the guardrail in question in a reasonably good state of repair." The trial court gave *Wis. J I-Civil, Part I,* 1005, defining negligence, but qualified that instruction as follows:

"A possessor has of premises upon which he has permitted a licensee to come or remain, must exercise ordinary care to the end that proper and timely warning may be given to the licenses of hidden dangers within or upon such premises.

"A possessor has no duty to discover dangers of which he is himself unaware. His duty only is to give proper and timely warning of those dangers which are known to him, and then only as to those dangers which he realizes or, in the exercise of ordinary care, should realize, involve an unreasonable risk of causing bodily harm to the licenses."

Answering the special verdict's questions, the jury found that Mahnke had no knowledge of the railing's defective condition and, hence, apportioned no negligence to Mahnke. Following motions after verdict, the Trial Court entered judgment on the verdict, dismissing the Pagelsdorfs' complaint. The plaintiffs appeal.

The question on which the appeal turns is whether the Trial Court erred in failing to instruct the jury that Mahnke owed Pagelsdorf a duty to exercise ordinary care in maintaining the premises.

Prior to December 10, 1975, the duty or an occupier of land toward visitors on the premises was determined in Wisconsin law on a sliding scale according to the status of the visitor. To trespassers, land occupiers owed only the duty of refraining from willful and intentional injury. *Copeland v. Larson,* 46 Wis.2d 337, 341, 174 N.W.2d 745 (1970). A person who had permission to enter the land, but who went upon it for his own purposes rather than to further an interest of the possessor, was labeled a licensee. Toward a licensee, the occupier owed the limited duty of keeping the property safe from traps and avoiding active negligence. There was no obligation regarding dangers unknown to the possessor. Id. The highest duty—that of ordinary care—was owed to an invitee, one who entered the land upon business concerning the possessor and at his invitation. Id. at 342, 174 N.W.2d 745. In *Antoniewicz v. Reszczynski,* 70 Wis.2d 836,854-55,236 N.W.2d I, 10 (1975), we abolished, prospectively, the distinction between the different duties owed by an occupier to licensees and to invitees:

"It would appear, therefore, that there is little to commend the continued use of the categories of licensee or invitee in respect to the liability of the occupier of property. As we have noted, the factual distinctions between licensees and invitees are hazy and the law blurred. There is no reason why one who invites a guest to a party at his home should have less concern for that guest's safety than he has for the welfare of an insurance man who may come to the home to deliver a policy. Is the life or welfare of a friend who comes as a guest to be more lightly regarded than the life or welfare of a casual business acquaintance? To state the question is to answer it. There is no good reason why the business guest should be afforded greater protection than the social guest. Particularly in Wisconsin, where the economic-benefit theory has been discarded in respect to invitees, no logical basis for any dichotomy remains.

"While the common-law categories may have had some virtue under the feudal system of land tenures, when the lord of the land had complete and autocratic control of his property irrespective of harm to the community, such concept of land holding has long since vanished. We recognize numerous limitations upon the right to use real property, most of which are imposed by the police power."

The facts of the instant case arose before the *Antoniewicz* decision; the parties agree that the extent of Mahnke's duty toward Pagelsdorf turns on whether Pagelsdorf was an invitee or a licensee with respect to Mahnke. Pagelsdorf maintains he was Mahnke's invitee; if he was, the jury should have been instructed that Mahnke owed him a duty of ordinary care. The defendants contend that the Trial Court properly determined that Pagelsdorf was Mahnke's licensee and, therefore, properly instructed the jury that he owed Pagelsdorf only a duty to warn of known hazards.

These arguments overlook the effect on a landowner's common law duty upon transfer of the premises from the owner to a lessee. The classification of visitors identified the degree of duty of the possessor or occupier of the premises. 2 Harper and James, *The Law of Torts*, sec. 27.2, 1488 (1956). When the property is leased, the duty of the landlord was controlled by a different rule: that, with certain exceptions, a landlord is not liable for injuries to his tenants and their visitors resulting from defects in the premises. See, e.g., *Skrzypczak v. Konieczka*, 224 Wis. 455, 458, 272 N.W. 659 (1937). The general rule of non-liability was based on the concept of a lease as a conveyance of property and the consequent transfer of possession and control of the premises to the tenant. 2 Harper and James, *supra*, sec. 27.16 at 1506; Restatement (Second) of *Torts*, sec. 356, Comment as (1965).

There are exceptions to this general rule of non-liability. The landlord is liable for injuries to the tenant or his visitor caused by a dangerous condition if he contracts to repair defects, or if, knowing of a defect existing at the time the tenant took possession, he conceals it from a tenant who could not reasonably be expected to discover it. *Skrzypczak v. Konieczka, supra;* Kurtz v. Pauly, 158 Wis. 534, 538-39, 149 N.W. 143 (1914); *Flood v. Pabst Brewing Co.,* 158 Wis. 626, 631-32, 149 N.W. 489 (1914). Additionally, the general rule is not applicable where the premises are leased for public use, or are retained in the landlord's control, or where the landlord negligently makes repairs. Restatement (Second) of *Torts,* secs. 859-62 (1965). The rule of non-liability persists despite a decided trend away from application of the general rule and toward expansion of its exceptions. Restatement (Second) of *Property,* (Tentative Draft No.4), Ch. 16 (1976); Restatement (Second) of Torts, secs. 855-56 (1965).

None of the exceptions to the general rule are applicable to the facts of this case. The premises were not leased for public use, nor was the porch within Mahnke's control, nor did he negligently repair the railing. The plaintiffs argue that Mahnke contracted to repair defects; but according to Mrs. Blattner's testimony, Mahnke's promise extended only to items the Blattners reported as being in disrepair. Therefore, error cannot be predicated on the Trial Court's failure to give an instruction concerning Mahnke's constructive knowledge where the asserted contract was to repair defects of which Mahnke actually knew. Finally, the concealed-defect exception does not apply because there was no evidence that the dry rot existed in 1969 when the Blattners moved in and because Mrs. Blattner testified that she knew of the rot in the railing.

Therefore, if we were to follow the traditional rule, Pagelsdorf was not entitled to an instruction that Mahnke owed him a duty of ordinary care. We believe, however, that the better public policy lies in the abandonment of the general rule of non-liability and the adoption of a rule that a landlord is under a duty to exercise ordinary care in the maintenance of the premises.

Such a rule was adopted by the New Hampshire court in *Sargent v. Ross,* 113 N.H. 388, 308 A.2d 628 (1978). The plaintiff's four-year-old child fell to her death from an outdoor stairway of a residential building owned by the defendant. In a wrongful death action against the landlord, the plaintiff claimed the stairs were too steep and the railing inadequate. The jury awarded the plaintiff damages, and the landlord appealed from a judgment entered on the verdict. After eliminating the established exceptions to the rule of non-liability, the court concluded that the rule had nothing to recommend itself in a contemporary, urban society and ought to be abandoned. Instead, general principles of negligence should apply. The court stated that the "quasi-sovereignty of the landowner" had its genesis in "agrarian England of the Dark Ages." *Id.* 308 A.2d at 530.

Whatever justification the rule might once have had, there no longer seemed to be any reason to release landlords from a general duty of exercising ordinary care to prevent foreseeable harm. The court reasoned that the modern trend away from special immunities in Tort law and the recognition of an implied warranty of habitability in an apartment lease transaction argued in favor of abolishing the common law rule of non-liability. Accordingly, a landlord's conduct should be appraised according to negligence principles. Questions of control, hidden defects, and common use would be relevant only if bearing on the general determination of negligence, including foreseeability and unreasonableness of the risk of harm.

[2] In *Antoniewicz, supra,* 70 Wis.2d at 850, n.2, 236 N.W.2d 1, we cited *Sargent* as one of many cases whose reasoning supported the abolition of the common law distinctions between licensees and invitees. The policies supporting our decision to abandon these distinctions concerning a land occupier's duty toward his visitors compel us, in the instant case, to abrogate the landlord's general cloak of immunity toward his tenants and their visitors. Having recognized that modern social conditions no longer support special exceptions for land occupiers, it is but a short step to hold that there is no remaining basis for a general rule of non-liability for landlords. Arguably, the landlord's relinquishment of possession, and consequently control of the premises, removes this case from the sweep of the policies embodied in *Antoniewicz*. We are not so persuaded. One of the basic principles of our Tort law is that one is liable for injuries resulting

from conduct foreseeably creating an unreasonable risk to others. *Osborne v. Montgomery,* 203 Wis. 223, 234 N.W. 372 (1931). Public policy limitations on the application of this principle are shrinking. See. e. g.: *Antoniewicz v. Reszczynski, supra,* (limited duty of occupier toward "licensees"); *Goller v. White,* 20 Wis.2d 402, 122 N.W.2d 193 (1963) (parental immunity); *Widell v. Holy Trinity Catholic Church,* 19 Wis.2d 648, 121 N.W.2d 249 (1963) (religious immunity); *Holytz v. Milwaukee,* 17 Wis.2d 26, 115 N.W.2d 618 (1962) (governmental immunity); *Kojis v. Doctors Hospital,* 12 Wis.2d 367, 107 N.W.2d 131, 107 N.W.2d 292 (1961) (charitable immunity).

[3] The modern-day apartment lease is regarded as a contract, not a conveyance. *Pines v. Perssion,* 14 Wis.2d 590, 111 N.W.2d 409 (1961). In *Pines,* we determined that modern social conditions called for judicial recognition of a warranty of habitability implied in an apartment lease:

"Legislation and administrative rules, such the safe-place statute, building codes, and health regulations, all impose certain duties on a property owner with respect to the condition of his premises. Thus, the legislature has made a policy judgment—that it is socially (and politically) desirable to impose these duties on a property owner— which has rendered the old common-law rule obsolete. To follow the old rule of no implied warranty of habitability in leases would, in our opinion, be inconsistent with the current legislative policy concerning housing standards. The need and social desirability of adequate housing for people in this era of rapid population increases is too important to be rebuffed by that obnoxious cliché, *caveat emptor.* Permitting landlords to rent "tumble-down" houses is at least a contributing cause of such problems as urban blight, juvenile delinquency, and high property taxes for conscientious landowners." *Id.* at 595-96, 111 N.W.2d at 412.

It would be anomalous indeed to require a landlord to keep his premises in good repair as an implied condition of the lease, yet immunize him from liability for injuries resulting from his failure to do so. We conclude that there is no remaining justification for the landlord's general cloak of common law immunity and hereby abolish the general common law principle of non-liability of landlords toward persons injured because of their defective premises.

At trial, plaintiffs' counsel requested the jury be instructed that Mahnke owed Pagelsdorf, as his invitee, a duty of ordinary care. Pagelsdorf's proposed special verdict inquired whether Mahnke was "negligent in failing to keep the guardrail in question in a reasonably good state of repair." Thus, Pagelsdorf preserved the assigned error for appeal. We simply reach the result he seeks by a different means. Cf.: *Haumschild v. Continental Casualty Co., 7* Wis.2d 130,141-42, 95 N.W.2d 814 (1959).

[4, 5] We have considered whether the rule we adopt today was so strongly implied in *Antoniewicz* that it might be unfair, in light of the prospective operation of that holding, to apply it to these facts that occurred before that decision. While the instant holding is a natural outgrowth of *Antoniewicz*, we believe the rule abrogated herein is distinguishable from *Antoniewicz* because the rule governing landlord liability was predicated on lack of control over the premises. Accordingly, the application of the new standard to landlord liability is not governed by the prospective operation of *Antoniewicz*. Nor are we persuaded that the rule adopted herein should operate prospectively only. Generally, a decision overruling or repudiating other eases is given retrospective operation. *Fitzgerald v. Meissner & Hicks, Inc.,* 38 Wis.2d 571, 575, 157 N.W.2d 595 (1968). The rule of landlords' non-liability was riddled with many exceptions; thus, reliance on the rule could not have been great. See; *Love, Landlord's Liability for Defective Premises: Caveat Lessee, Negligence, or Strict Liability?, 1975 Wis.L.Rev. 19, 116-17.* We find no reason to depart from the general rule of retrospective operation of the mandate herein.

[6] In conclusion, a landlord owes his tenant or anyone on the premises with the tenant's consent a duty to exercise ordinary care. If a person lawfully on the premises is injured because of the landlord's negligence in maintaining the premises, he is entitled to recover from the landlord under general negligence principles. Issues of notice of the defect, its obviousness, control of the premises, and so forth are all relevant only insofar as they bear on the ultimate question: Did the landlord exercise ordinary care in the maintenance of the premises under all the circumstances?

Judgment reversed and cause remanded for proceedings consistent with this opinion.

COFFEY, J., not participating.

PAGELSDORF v. SAFECO INS. CO. OF AMERICA
Cite as Wis. 284 N.W. 2d 55

Your Brief

_____

_____

_____

_____

_____

_____

_____

_____

_____

_____

_____

Model Brief

Pagelsdorf v. Safeco

Facts:
A tenant, at the defendant's apartment complex, invited a friend to help move furniture out of her apartment. While lifting the furniture over the railing on the balcony, the railing gave way and the friend was injured. The tenant and landlord had an oral agreement that the landlord must make all necessary repairs on the premises. The landlord testified at the trial that when he examined the railings after the accident, he noticed that the railing had dry-rotted inside, thus a concealed danger. The friend sued the landlord, alleging that he was owed a duty by the landlord, and that the landlord breached his duty by not exercising ordinary care in the maintenance of his premises. The defendant argued that his duty does not extend to the invitee of a tenant.

Issue:
Whether the trial court erred in failing to instruct the jury that a landlord owed a duty to the plaintiff in exercising ordinary care in the maintenance of its premises. Does a landlord's duty of care extend to those on the premises who are not tenants?

Proceedings Below:
The Trial Court submitted instructions to the jury that did not include the landlord's duty to exercise ordinary care to an invitee of the tenant. Rather, the instructions simply addressed the landlord's duty to discover potential dangers. The jury did not find negligence on behalf of the landlord. The plaintiff appealed based on the Trial Court's omission of an instruction that would have caused the jury to rule on the landlord's duty to exercise ordinary care toward him, an invitee.

Holding:

The Court of Appeals found that a landlord must exercise ordinary care toward its tenant and others on the premises with permission. It, therefore, reversed and remanded the case to the lower court for proceedings consistent with its reasoning.

Reason for Decision:

The court stated that modern landlord tenant law imposes on the landlord a duty to keep the premises in good repair. The court reasoned that it would not make sense to require a landlord to keep his premises in good repair as an implied condition of the lease, yet immunize him from liability for injuries resulting from his failure to do so. Thus, the court held that a landlord has a duty to exercise ordinary care toward tenants and others rightfully on the premises.

Constitutional Law

OCTOBER TERM, 1977

Syllabus

ZABLOCKI, MILWAUKEE COUNTY CLERK
v.
REDHAIL

APPEAL FROM THE UNITED STATES DISTRICT COURT FOR THE EASTERN DISTRICT OF WISCONSIN

No. 76-879.
Argued October 4, 1977.
Decided January 18, 1978.

Wisconsin statute providing that any resident of that state "having minor issue not in his custody and which he is under obligation to support by any court order, or judgment" may not marry without a court approval order, which cannot be granted absent showing that the support obligation has not been met and that children covered by the support order "are not then, and are not likely thereafter to become public charges," *held* to violate the Equal Protection Clause of the Fourteenth Amendment. Pp. 383-391.

(a) Since the right to marry is of fundamental importance, e.g., *Loving v. Virginia*, 388 U.S. 1, and the statutory classification involved here significantly interferes with the exercise of that right, "critical examination" of the state interests advanced in support of the classification is required. *Massachusetts Board of Retirement v. Murgia*, 427 U. S. 307, 312, 314. Pp. 383-387.

(b) The state interests assertedly served by the challenged statute unnecessarily impinge on the right to marry. If the statute is designed to furnish all opportunity to counsel persons with prior child-support obligations before further such obligations are incurred, it neither expressly requires counseling nor provides for automatic approval after counseling is completed. The statute cannot be justified as encouraging an applicant to support his children. By the proceeding the state, which already possesses numerous other means for exacting compliance with support obligations, merely prevents the applicant from getting married, without ensuring support of the applicant's prior children. Though it is suggested that the statute protects the ability of marriage applicants to meet prior support obligations before new ones are incurred, the statute is both under-inclusive (as it does not limit new financial commitments other than those arising out of the contemplated marriage) and over-inclusive (since the new spouse may better the applicant's financial situation). Pp. 388-390.

418 F. Supp. 1061,   *affirmed.*

ZABLOCKI v. REDHAIL

Opinion of the Court

MARSHALL, J., delivered the opinion of the Court, in which BURGER, C. J., and BRENNAN, WHITE, BLACKMUN, J. J., joined. BURGER, C. J., filed a concurring opinion, *post*, p. 391. STEWART, J., *post*, p. 391, POWELL, J., *post*, p. 396, and STEVENS, J, *post*, p. 403, filed opinions concurring in the judgment. REHNQUIST, J., filed a dissenting opinion, *post*, p. 407.

Ward L. Johnson Jr., Assistant Attorney General of Wisconsin, argued the cause for appellant. With him on the briefs were *Bronson C. La Follette* Attorney General, *Robert P Russell*, and *John R. Devitt*.

Robert H. Blondis argued the cause and filed briefs for appellee.*

MR. JUSTICE MARSHALL delivered the opinion of the Court.

At issue in this case is the constitutionality of a Wisconsin statute, Wis. Stat. §§ 245.10 (1), (4), (5) (1973), which provides that members of a certain class of Wisconsin residents may not marry, within the state or elsewhere, without first obtaining a court order granting permission to marry. The class is defined by the statute to include any "Wisconsin resident having minor issue not in his custody and which he is under obligation to support by any court order or judgment." The statute specifies that court permission cannot be granted unless the marriage applicant submits proof of compliance with the support obligation and, in addition, demonstrates that the children covered by the support order "are not then and are not likely thereafter to become public charges." No marriage license may lawfully be issued in Wisconsin to a person covered by the statute, except upon

court order; any marriage entered into without compliance with §
245.10 is declared void; and persons acquiring marriage licenses in
violation of the section are subject to criminal penalties.

OCTOBER TERM, 1977

Opinion of the Court

After being denied a marriage license because of his failure
to comply with § 245.10, appellee brought this class action under
42 U.S.C. § 1983, challenging the statute as violative of the Equal
Protection and Due Process Clauses of the Fourteenth Amendment
and seeking declaratory and injunctive relief. The United States District Court for the Eastern District of Wisconsin held the statute
unconstitutional under the Equal Protection Clause and enjoined
its enforcement. 418 F. Supp. 1061 (1976). We noted probable jurisdiction, 429 U. S. 1089 (1977), and we now affirm.

I

Appellee Redhail is a Wisconsin resident who, under the terms of
§ 245.10, is unable to enter into a lawful marriage in Wisconsin or
elsewhere so long as he maintains his Wisconsin residency. The facts,
according to the stipulation filed by the parties in the District Court,
are as follows. In January 1972, when appellee was a minor and a
high school student, a paternity action was instituted against him in
Milwaukee County Court, alleging that he was the father of a baby
girl born out of wedlock on July 5, 1971. After he appeared and admitted that he was the child's father, the court entered an order on
May 12, 1972, adjudging appellee the father and ordering him to pay
$109 per month as support for the child until she reached eighteen
years of age. From May 1972 until August 1974, appellee was un-
employed and indigent, and consequently was unable to make any
support payments.

On September 27, 1974, appellee filed an application for a marriage license with appellant Zablocki, the county clerk of Milwaukee County, and a few days later the application was denied on the sole ground that appellee had not obtained a court order granting him permission to marry, as required by § 245.10. Although appellee did not petition a state court thereafter, it is stipulated that he would not have been able to satisfy either of the statutory prerequisites for an order granting permission to marry. First, he had not satisfied his support obligations to his illegitimate child, and as of December 1974, there was an arrearage in excess of $3,700. Second, the child had been a public charge since her birth, receiving benefits under the Aid to Families with Dependent Children program. It is stipulated that the child's benefit payments were such that she would have been a public charge even if appellee had been current in his support payments.

On December 24, 1974, appellee filed his complaint in the District Court, on behalf of himself and the class of all Wisconsin residents who had been refused a marriage license pursuant to § 245.10(1) by one of the county clerks in Wisconsin. Zablocki was named as the defendant, individually and as representative of a class consisting of all county clerks in the state. The complaint alleged, among other things, that appellee and the woman he desired to marry were expecting a child in March 1975 and wished to be lawfully married before that time. The statute was attacked on the grounds that it deprived appellee, and the class he sought to represent, of equal protection and due process rights secured by the First, Fifth, Ninth, and Fourteenth Amendments to the United States Constitution.

A three-judge court was convened pursuant to 28 U. S. C. §§ 2281, 2284. Appellee moved for certification of the plaintiff and defendant classes named in his complaint, and by order dated February 20, 1975, the plaintiff class was certified under Fed. Rule Civ. Proc. 23 (b)(2). After the parties filed the stipulation of facts, and briefs on the merits, oral argument was heard in the District Court on June 23,

1975, with a representative from the Wisconsin Attorney General's office participating in addition to counsel for the parties.

The three-judge court handed down a unanimous decision on August 31, 1976. The court ruled, first, that it was not required to abstain from decision under the principles set forth in *Huffman v. Pursue, Ltd.*, 420 U. S. 592 (1975), and *Younger v. Harris*, 401 U.S. 37 (1971), since there was no pending state-court proceeding that could be frustrated by the declaratory and injunctive relief requested. Second, the court held that the class of all county clerks in Wisconsin was a proper defendant class under Rules 23 (a) and (b)(2), and that neither Rule 23 nor due process required prejudgment notice to the members of the plaintiff or the defendant class.

On the merits, the three-judge panel analyzed the challenged statute under the Equal Protection Clause and concluded that "strict scrutiny" was required because the classification created by the statute infringed upon a fundamental right, the right to marry. The court then proceeded to evaluate the interests advanced by the state to justify the statute, and, finding that the classification was not necessary for the achievement of those interests, the court held the statute invalid and enjoined the county clerks from enforcing it.

Appellant brought this direct appeal pursuant to 28 U.S.C. § 1253, claiming that the three-judge court erred in finding §§24.10 (1), (4), (5) invalid under the Equal Protection clause. Appellee defends the lower court's equal protection holding and, in the alternative, urges affirmance of the District Court's judgment on the ground that the statute does not satisfy the requirements of substantive due process. We agree with the District Court that the statute violates the Equal Protection Clause.

II

In evaluating §§ 245.10 (1), (4), (5) under the Equal Protection Clause, "we must first determine what burden of justification the classification created thereby must meet, by looking to the nature of the classification and the individual interests affected." *Memorial Hospital v. Maricopa County,* 415 U. S. 250, 253 (1974). Since our past decisions make clear that the right to marry is of fundamental importance, and since the classification at issue here significantly interferes with the exercise of that right, we believe that "critical examination" of the state interests advanced in support of the classification is required. *Massachusetts Board of Retirement v. Murgia,* 427 U. S. 307, 312, 314 (1976); see, e.g., *San Antonio Independent School Dist. v. Rodriquez,* 411 U. S. 1, 17 (1973).

The leading decision of this court on the right to marry is *Loving v. Virginia,* 388 U. S. 1 (1967). In that case, an interracial couple who had been convicted of violating Virginias miscegenation laws challenged the statutory scheme on both equal protection and due process grounds. The court's opinion could have rested solely on the ground that the statutes discriminated based on race in violation of the Equal Protection Clause. *Id.,* at 11-12. But the court went on to hold that the laws arbitrarily deprived the couple of a fundamental liberty protected by the Due Process Clause, the freedom to marry. The court's language on the latter point bears repeating:

"The freedom to marry has long been recognized as one of the vital personal rights essential to the orderly pursuit of happiness by free men.

"Marriage is one of the 'basic civil rights of man,' fundamental to our very existence and survival." *Id.,* at 12, quoting *Skinner v. Oklahoma ex rel. Williamson,* 316 U. S. 535, 541 (1942).

Although *Loving* arose in the context of racial discrimination, prior and subsequent decisions of this court confirm that the right to marry is of fundamental importance for all individuals. Long ago, in *Maynard v. Hill,* 125 U. S. 190 (1888), the court characterized marriage as "the most important relation in life," *Id.,* at 205, and as "the foundation of the family and of society, without which there would be neither civilization nor progress," *Id*, at 211. In *Meyer v. Nebraska*, 262 U. S. 390 (1923), the court recognized that the right "to marry, establish a home and bring up children" is a central part of the liberty protected by the Due Process Clause, *Id.*, at 399, and in *Skinner v. Oklahoma ex rel. Williamson, supra,* marriage was described as "fundamental to the very existence and survival of the race," 316 U.S. at 541.

More recent decisions have established that the right to marry is part of the fundamental "right of privacy" implicit in the Fourteenth Amendments' Due Process Clause. In *Griswold v. Connecticut,* 381 U. S. 479 (1965), the Court observed:

"We deal with a right of privacy older than the Bill of Rights— older than our political parties, older than our school system. Marriage is a coming together for better or for worse, hopefully enduring, and intimate to the degree of being sacred. It is an association that promotes a way of life, not causes; a harmony in living, not political faiths; a bilateral loyalty, not commercial or social projects. Yet it is an association for as noble a purpose as any involved in our prior decisions." *Id.*, at 486.

See also, *Id.,* at 495 (Goldberg, J., concurring); Id. at 502-503 (White, J. concurring in judgment).

Cases subsequent to *Griswold* and *Loving* have routinely categorized the decision to marry as among the personal decisions protected by the right of privacy. See generally, *Whalen v. Roe,* 429 U. S. 589, 598-600 and in 23-26 (1977). For example, last Term in *Carey v. Population Services International,* 431 U. S. 678 (1977), we declared;

"While the outer limits of [the right of personal privacy] have not been marked by the Court, it is clear that among the decisions that an individual may make without unjustified government interference are personal decisions 'relating to marriage, *Loving v. Virginia,* 388 U. S. 1, 12, (1967); procreation, *Skinner v. Oklahoma ex rel.* Williamson, 316 U. S. 535, 541-542 (1942); contraception, *Eisenstadt v. Baird,* 405 U. S. at 453-454; *Id.* at 460, 463-465 (White, J. concurring in result); family relationships, *Prince v. Massachusetts,* 321 U. S. 158, 166, (1944); and child rearing and education, *Pierce v. Society of Sisters,* 208 U. S. 510, 535 (1925); *Meyer v. Nebraska* [262 U. S. 390, 399 (1923)]." *Id.,* at 684-685, quoting Roe v. Wade, 410 U. S. 113, 152-153 (1973).

See also *Cleveland Board of Education v. LaFleur,* 414 U. S. 632, 639-640 (1974) ("This Court has long recognized that freedom of personal choice in matters of marriage and family life is one of the liberties protected by the Due Process Clause of the Fourteenth Amendment"); *Smith v. Organization of Foster Families,* 431 U. S. 816, 842-844 (1977); *Moore v. East Cleveland,* 431 U. S. 494, 499 (1977); *Paul v. Davis,* 424 U. S. 693, 713 (1976).

It is not surprising that the decision to marry is on the same level of importance as decisions relating to procreation, childbirth, child rearing, and family relationships. As the facts of this case illustrate, it would make little sense to recognize a right of privacy with respect to other matters of family life and not with respect to the decision to enter the relationship that is the foundation of the family in our society. The woman whom appellee desired to marry had a fundamental right to seek an abortion of their expected child, see *Roe v. Wade, supra,* or to bring the child into life to suffer the myriad social, if not economic disabilities that the status of illegitimacy brings, see *Trimble v. Gordon,* 403 U .S. 762, 768-770, and n. 13 (1977); *Weber v. Aetna Casualty & Surety Co.,* 406 U. S. 164, 175-176 (1972). Surely, a decision to marry and raise the child in a traditional family setting must receive equivalent protection. And, if appellee's right to procreate means anything at all, it must imply some right to enter the only relationship in which the State of Wisconsin allows sexual relations legally to take place.

By reaffirming the fundamental character of the right to marry, we do not mean to suggest that every state regulation that relates in any way to the incidents of or prerequisites for marriage must be subjected to rigorous scrutiny. To the contrary, reasonable regulations that do not significantly interfere with the decision to enter into the marital relationship may legitimately be imposed. See *Califano v. Jobst, ante,* p. 47; n. 12, *infra.* The statutory classification at issue here, however, clearly does interfere directly and substantially with the right to marry.

Under the challenged statute, no Wisconsin resident in the affected class may marry in Wisconsin or elsewhere without a court order, and marriages contracted in violation of the statute are both void and punishable as criminal offenses. Some of those in the affected class, like appellee, will never be able to obtain the necessary court order, because they either lack the financial means to meet their support obligations or cannot prove that their children will not become public charges. These persons are absolutely prevented from getting married. Many others, able in theory to satisfy the statutes requirements, will be sufficiently burdened by having to do so that they will in effect be coerced into forgoing their right to marry. And even those who can be persuaded to meet the statutes' requirements, suffer a serious intrusion into their freedom of choice in an area in which we have held such freedom to be fundamental.

When a statutory classification significantly interferes with the exercise of a fundamental right, it cannot be upheld unless it is supported by sufficiently important state interests and is closely tailored to effectuate only those interests. See, e.g., *Carey v. Population Services International,* 431 U. S. at 686; *Memorial Hospital v. Maricopa County,* 415 U. S. at 262-263; *San Antonio Independent School Dist. v. Rodriguez,* 411 U. S. at 16-17; *Ballock v. Carter,* 405 U. S. 134, 144 (1972). Appellant asserts that the challenged statute serves two interests: the permission-to-marry proceeding furnishes an opportunity to counsel the applicant as to the necessity of fulfilling his prior support obligations; and the welfare of the out-of-custody children is protected. We may accept for present purposes that these are legitimate and substantial interests, but, since the means selected by the state for achieving these interests unnecessarily impinge on the right to marry, the statute cannot be sustained.

There is evidence that the challenged statute, as originally introduced in the Wisconsin Legislature, was intended merely to establish a mechanism whereby persons with support obligations to children from prior marriages could be counseled before they entered into new marital relationships and incurred further support obligations. Court permission to marry was to be required, but apparently, permission was automatically to be granted after counseling was completed. The statute actually enacted, however, does not expressly require or provide for any counseling whatsoever, nor for any automatic granting of permission to marry by the court, and thus it can hardly be justified as a means for ensuring counseling of the persons within its coverage. Even assuming that counseling does take place— a fact as to which there is no evidence in the record—this interest obviously cannot support the withholding of a court permission to marry once counseling is completed.

With regard to safeguarding the welfare of the out-of-custody children, appellant's brief does not make clear the connection between the state's interest and the statute's requirements. At argument, appellant's counsel suggested that, since permission to marry cannot be granted unless the applicant shows that he has satisfied his court-determined support obligations to the prior children and that those children will not become public charges, the statute provides incentive for the applicant to make support payments to his children. Tr. of Oral Arg. 17-20. This "collection device" rationale cannot justify the statute's broad infringement on the right to marry.

First, with respect to individuals who are unable to meet the statutory requirements, the statute merely prevents the applicant from getting married, without delivering any money at all into the hands of the applicant's prior children. More importantly, regardless of the applicant's ability or willingness to meet the statutory requirements, the state already has numerous other means for exacting compliance with support obligations, means that are at least as effective as the instant statute's and yet do not impinge upon the right to marry. Under Wisconsin law, whether the children are from a prior marriage or were born out of wedlock, courtdetermined support obligations may be enforced directly via wage assignments, civil contempt proceedings, and criminal penalties. And, if the state believes that parents of children out of their custody should be responsible for ensuring that those children do not become public charges, this interest can be achieved by adjusting the criteria used for determining the amounts to be paid under their support orders.

There is also some suggestion that §245.10 protects the ability of marriage applicants to meet support obligations to prior children by preventing the applicants from incurring new support obligations. But the challenged provisions of §245.10 are grossly under-inclusive with respect to this purpose, since they do not limit in any way new financial commitments by the applicant other than those arising out of the contemplated marriage. The statutory classification is substantially over-inclusive as well: Given the possibility that the new spouse will actually better the applicant's financial situation, by contributing income from a job or otherwise, the statute in many cases may prevent affected individuals from improving their ability to satisfy their prior support obligations. And, although it is true that the applicant will incur support obligations to any children born during the contemplated marriage, preventing the marriage may only result in the children being born out of wedlock, as in fact occurred in appellee's case. Since the support obligation is the same whether the child is born in or out of wedlock, the net result of preventing the marriage is simply more illegitimate children.

The statutory classification created by §§245.10 (1), (4), (5) thus cannot be justified by the interests advanced in support of it. The judgment of the District Court is, accordingly,

Affirmed.

Your Brief

_____

_____

_____

_____

_____

_____

_____

_____

_____

_____

_____

_____

Model Brief

Zablocki v. Redhail, **434 U. S. 374**

Facts:
Appellee Redhail is a Wisconsin resident who was denied the right
to marry under a Wisconsin statute, because he had failed to comply
with his support obligations of his minor child. That statute provided
that as long as he maintained his Wisconsin residency, he would not
be able to marry in Wisconsin or elsewhere until he had satisfied his
delinquent child support obligations.

Appellee brought this class action to declare the Wisconsin statute unconstitutional under the Equal Protection and Due Process
Clauses of the Fourteenth Amendment to the Constitution.

Issues:
The issue presented in this case is whether the Wisconsin statute violated the Equal Protection Clause of the Fourteenth Amendment.

Proceedings Below:
The U.S. District Court held that the statute violated the Equal Protection Clause because the statute violated the fundamental right to
marry. The court also concluded that the state interests sought to be
achieved by the statute did not justify the violation of the appellee's
fundamental right to marry.

Holding:
The Supreme Court affirmed the District Court, and held that
the Wisconsin statute violates the Equal Protection Clause of the
Fourteenth Amendment and could not be justified by the interests
advanced in support of it.

Reasoning:

In concluding that the Wisconsin statute violated the Equal Protection Clause, the court reasoned as follows:

1. The right to marry is part of the fundamental right of privacy; therefore any statute that *significantly* interferes with that right must be critically examined, i.e., subject to strict scrutiny.

2. The court found that the Wisconsin statute *significantly* interfered with the right to marry because under the statute no Wisconsin resident in the affected class could marry in Wisconsin or elsewhere without a court order. Furthermore, any marriages entered into in violation of the statute are both void and punishable as criminal offenses.

The court also noted, however, that state regulations that do not *significantly* interfere with the right to marry may be legitimately imposed.

3. After having found that the Wisconsin statute significantly interfered with the fundamental right to marry, the court found that the statute could be upheld only if it is supported by compelling state interests and closely tailored to effectuate only those interests.

4. The interests sought to be furthered by the statute were: (a) the opportunity to counsel marriage applicants who were delinquent in their support obligations as to the necessity of meeting those obligations and (b) protecting the welfare of the out-of-custody child.

5. The court found that these were legitimate interests but not compelling and that the means selected to enforce these interests unnecessarily impinged on the right to marry. The court found that the statute did not expressly or otherwise provide for counseling of the marriage applicant as to their support obligations and thus could not be justified on those grounds.

As to the state interest regarding the "welfare of the child," the court found that the statute was not justified as a collections device because the state did not deliver any money to the marriage applicant's out-of-custody children. Furthermore, the state had numerous other and more effective means for collection, including wage assignments, civil contempt proceedings, and criminal penalties.

6. The court also found that the statute was not effective in preventing the marriage applicant from incurring further support obligations because the statute did not limit financial commitments by the applicant other than those arising out of the contemplated marriage.

The court further reasoned that the new spouse of the marriage applicant might, in some cases, improve the applicant's financial situation, and thus enable him or her to meet his or her delinquent child support obligations. Finally, the court reasoned that although the marriage applicant will incur support obligations to any children born in the contemplated marriage, preventing the marriage may result in any children being born out of wedlock, which was the case with one of the members of the affected class suing the state. Hence, the court concluded that the net result of the statute may be more illegitimate children.

Note: In Zablocki v. Redhail *there were separate concurring opinions written by Chief Justice Burger, Justice Stewart, Justice Powell, Justice Stevens, and a dissenting opinion by Justice Renquist. However, for the purposes of this exercise we have only discussed the opinion delivered for the court by Justice Marshall.*

7 | THINKING LIKE A LAWYER: APPLYING CASE PRECEDENT

A big part of "thinking like a lawyer" is being able to understand how the holding in one case can be applied to a different set of facts in a second case. This is called citing "case precedent." In law school, you learn how to cite case precedent to argue for or against a certain proposition. Because this is such an important part of what you learn in law school, we wanted to give you a dry run of how law students and lawyers do this, so that again, you can see if you find this type of exercise challenging and interesting.

Since you need cases to cite, we're going to use the five cases you've just briefed. Here's a sample to get you started.

Sample Exercise

First, reread the facts in our sample brief, *The People of Michigan v. Graham Donit*. Then, read the following case summary:

People of Illinois v. Murray Green

Murray Green was arrested for the murder of Joe Brown while Murray was robbing Joe's grocery store. The police apprehended and arrested Murray close to the scene of the crime. While the arresting officer was reading Murray his rights, Murray proceeded to taunt the officer, calling him a low life pig. The officer immediately stopped reading Murray his rights, beat him up, tagged him with a stun gun, and then put him in the squad car. Subsequently, Murray was never read his rights.

The defense attorney argued that the murder charges should be dismissed against Murray because he had never been read his rights. The prosecution cited our sample case, *The People of Michigan v. Graham Donit,* and argued that Murray's taunting words to the police constituted a waiver of his rights and thus the murder charges against Murray should not be dismissed.

What would the court hold?

ANSWER

The primary issue is whether the facts in our sample case above are similar enough to the facts in *The People of Michigan v. Graham Donit* to mandate that the court should have the same holding. Let's carefully examine the key facts. In the Graham Donit case, the defendant taunted the police officer by "reciting *his rights* himself" before the police officer could.

Because the defendant recited his rights, the court held that he was aware of and knowledgeable about his rights. Thus, although the police officer did not read the defendant his rights, the court held that the defendant had knowingly waived that requirement by reciting them himself.

In the above case, the defendant taunted the police officer, not by reciting his rights, but by verbally abusing the officer. At no time, however, did the defendant recite his rights. The decision in the Graham case turned on the defendant's recitation of *his* rights to the police officer, not on the fact that he taunted the police officer with words that had nothing to do with the recitation of his rights. Thus, the court in the above case could *distinguish* the Graham case and hold that the charges against Murray should be dismissed because: (1) he had never been read his rights and (2) although he taunted the police officer, those taunts did not constitute a knowing waiver of such rights.

In the following exercise, you'll look at fact patterns from cases that cited one of the five cases that you briefed. You'll then answer a question that will require you to understand how the court's holding in the first case can apply to the second case.

For this exercise, it's important to revisit each of the five cases you have just briefed: *Calder v. Jones, Brand v. Prince, Larese v. Creamland Dairies, Inc., Pagelsdorf v. Safeco* and *Zablocki v. Redhail*.

Read the summaries provided for each of the following cases and use those facts to determine how they could be used to support or distinguish the above cases.

Civil Procedure

1.) Reread the brief for *Calder v. Jones*.
2.) Read the summary provided for *Retail Software v. Hal Lashlee*.
3.) Answer the question that follows the case summary.

Case Summary

Retail Software

v.

Hal Lashlee, 854 F.2D 18

The plaintiff, Retail Software Service (Retail), was a New York corporation. It brought a claim of fraud, breach of fiduciary duty, and violations of the civil racketeering statute (RICO), against the defendant, SCI, a California corporation, and against individuals associated with SCI. Those individuals are California residents.

The defendants, through SCI Corporation, regularly conducted business in New York, registered and solicited franchise sales there, and eventually sold seven franchises in the state. Retail alleges that SCI caused injury when it was purposely misled, at a California meeting, about the financial health of SCI, and intentionally misinformed about material facts relating to the franchise sale in New York. When SCI later filed for bankruptcy, Retail had already deposited $187,000 toward the purchase of the franchises and had incurred other costs (all in direct response to the misrepresentations). As a result, Retail filed suit in a New York court against the individuals of SCI.

The defendants moved to have the case in New York dismissed for lack of personal jurisdiction. They argued that they were not subject to the personal jurisdiction of a New York court because that would "offend traditional notions of fair play and substantial justice"

The District Court held that personal jurisdiction could not be asserted simply because the defendants were affiliated with a company that engaged in sales in New York. The District Court went on to state that simply operating a franchise does not create sufficient ties or contacts to New York to try them in a New York court. On appeal, the Court of Appeals reversed and remanded the case.

In overruling the lower court decision, the Court of Appeals followed *Calder v. Jones,* and stated that *Retail* was an even clearer example of why personal jurisdiction should be found.

If you are writing the majority opinion for the U.S. Court of Appeals, how would you argue that *Calder v. Jones* supports a finding of personal jurisdiction in the *Retail* case?

Your Answer

_____

_____

_____

_____

_____

_____

_____

_____

_____

_____

_____

_____

_____

_____

Model Answer

The litigated issue in both *Calder v. Jones* and in *Retail Software Services. Inc. v. Lashlee* centers on whether a court can assert personal jurisdiction over non-resident defendants. In both cases, the courts cited "traditional notions of fair play and substantial justice" as factors or elements to consider in determining whether the assertion of personal jurisdiction is proper.

In *Calder,* the court, in finding that the defendants were subject to the personal jurisdiction of a California court, noted that they knew their actions in Florida (writing and publishing the article) would have an effect in California and on the plaintiff, and he knew that the *National Enquirer* has its largest circulation in California. Because the defendants knew or should have known that their actions would cause injury in California, based upon the effect and fallout of the story, the court found that an assertion of personal jurisdiction was proper.

Calder can be used to support a finding of personal jurisdiction in *Retail* because the defendants also should have known that their California conduct would have an effect in New York. They intentionally sold franchises in New York, intentionally misled the plaintiffs to encourage the sale in New York, and purposely misrepresented material information, again to encourage a sale in New York. Thus, as in *Calder,* the defendants' actions clearly had an intentional tortious impact in New York. Because the injury was foreseeable, personal jurisdiction should be found.

* If you also noted in your answer that, even more than in *Calder,* the defendants had economic ties in New York, thereby creating a greater tie to the state and an additional basis for finding personal jurisdiction as did the court in *Retail,* you are well on your way to becoming a top law school student!

Property

1.) Reread the brief for *Brand v. Prince*.
2.) Read the summary provided for *Perez v. Perez*.
3.) Follow the instructions at the end of the case summary.

Case Summary

Perez
v.
Perez, 588 NYS 173

The husband and wife were divorced. The husband (defendant) claimed that he was entitled to certain marital real property based on a claim of adverse possession.

The wife disputes his claim arguing that he possessed the property in full recognition of her rights and, therefore, does not own the property by virtue of adverse possession.

The lower court denied the husband's motion for summary judgment, claiming that "a genuine issue of material fact" existed, i.e., whether his possession of the property had been hostile and under claim of right: Thus, whether he owned the property through adverse possession could not be conclusively determined. He appealed. In affirming the lower court's decision, the state Supreme Court cited and followed *Brand v. Prince*.

Explain how *Brand v. Prince* was controlling in the Supreme Court's decision not to grant the motion for summary judgment.

Your Answer

_____

_____

_____

_____

_____

_____

_____

_____

_____

_____

_____

_____

_____

_____

_____

_____

_____

_____

_____

_____

_____

_____

_____

_____

_____

_____

Model Answer

Brand v. Prince shows that to establish adverse possession, the following elements must be present. The plaintiff's possession of the property must be:

(1) open

(2) notorious

(3) hostile (to the defendant's interests)

(4) under claim of right (denying anyone else's right)

(5) exclusive

(6) continuous

Without the presence of all of these elements, i.e., if any one is absent, a court cannot find adverse possession.

To deny a motion for summary judgment, a court must find that a genuine issue of material fact exists. That is, if there is some factual uncertainty as to whether each element is present, a court cannot rule in favor of a summary judgment motion. In *Perez,* and in applying the elements enumerated in *Prince,* there is a question of whether the husband's possession was hostile and under claim of right. If, in fact, he possessed the property in full recognition of his former wife's existing interest and right, then his possession would be neither hostile nor under claim of right.

Thus, *Brand v. Prince* would be controlling because it elaborated a clear standard for a claim of adverse possession, and the facts in Perez clearly do not meet that standard.

Contracts

1.) Reread the brief of *Larese v. Creamland Dairies.*

2.) Read the summary provided for *Hubbard Chevrolet Co. v. General Motors Corporation.*

3.) Follow the instructions at the end of the case summary.

Case Summary

Hubbard Chevrolet Co.
v.
General Motors Corporation 873 F. 2d 873

Plaintiff Hubbard operated a car dealer franchise for General Motors (GM). Suffering from a downturn in sales, Hubbard requested from GM permission or consent to relocate his dealership. Under the terms of their dealership agreement, Hubbard could not change location without receiving GM's prior written approval. Although Hubbard had found an alternate site where he believed his sales would improve, GM refused to grant its consent.

Hubbard sued GM, claiming that an implied covenant of good faith and fair dealing existed to protect his reasonable expectation of receiving the necessary consent. Hubbard argued that by withholding consent, GM was violating this implied covenant.

A lower court jury returned a verdict in favor of Hubbard's claim, awarding him $2 million in damages for the breach of the implied covenant.

On appeal, the Court of Appeals reversed the jury verdict, citing precedent that held that unless the contract contains language that grants a party discretion to make a decision about whether to grant consent, no such discretion should be read into the contract. The court stated further that only the literal terms of the contract should be controlling. Thus, because the contract between Hubbard and GM did not contain such discretionary language and only said that GM shall give its prior consent, and according to the court, the contract's terms were "unmistakably expressed," the jury verdict was reversed. In its opinion, the court stated that not taking the literal meaning of the contract and reading into it discretionary language only as a "requirement of public policy...would be an extreme step for judges to take."

This case has now been appealed to the U.S. Supreme Court where it was granted a *writ of certiorari* based upon an unrelated constitutional issue. The Supreme Court affirms the Circuit Court's holding against reading into the contract a covenant of good faith and fair dealing.

As the lone dissenting justice, you must write a dissent citing *Larese v. Creamland Dairies.*

Your Answer

_____

_____

_____

_____

_____

_____

_____

_____

_____

_____

_____

_____

_____

_____

_____

_____

_____

_____

_____

_____

_____

_____

_____

_____

_____

_____

_____

_____

_____

_____

Model Answer

In affirming the Circuit Court's holding in *Hubbard v. GM,* this court supported the finding that judges and courts may not read an implied covenant of good faith and fair dealing into a contract that gives one party the right either to terminate the agreement or to grant consent. Further, this court affirms the notion that, absent explicit terms in the contract that provide discretion and create a reasonable expectation of reasonableness in deciding whether to grant consent, the court shall not supply such discretion. In essence, only a literal reading of a contract controls a court's actions.

The majority, however, fails to appreciate the reasoning of *Larese v. Creamland Dairies,* which states that a franchisor's consent cannot be "unreasonably" withheld under a franchise contract absent a provision stating explicitly that such consent can be withheld unreasonably.

That same standard and expectation of reasonableness found in the *Larese* case must apply here as well. Hubbard had a reasonable expectation to receive GM's consent since they had no explicit right to act unreasonably and withhold such consent. Just as the court held in *Larese,* every court should read into contracts a covenant of good faith and fair play, unless the parties specifically bargain for a right to act unreasonably. To hold otherwise not only contravenes the sound reasoning of the court in *Larese,* but also commonly held notions of sound public policy. I, therefore, dissent arguing that the standard of reasonableness articulated in *Larese v. Creamland Dairies* should control in this case as well.

Torts

1.) Reread the brief of *Pagelsdorf v. Safeco.*

2.) Read the summary provided for *Maci v. State Farm Fire and Casualty Co.*

3.) Follow the instructions at the end of the case summary.

Case Summary

Maci

v.

State Farm Fire and Casualty Co., 314 NW 917

Plaintiff Maci and his insurer brought suit against the landlord and his insurer for injuries sustained on the landlord's property.

In the early morning after a snowfall, the plaintiff slipped on an icy portion of the landlord's premises, sustained injuries, and filed suit claiming that the landlord had breached his duty of care. The premises had been shoveled earlier the prior evening, but impacted snow and ice remained, creating an unsafe situation.

Due to rules imposed by the landlord, the plaintiff had to walk along the icy portion of the property to go to his car. The plaintiff fell and suffered injuries while he was walking through that area.

The jury found that the landlord had breached his duty of care and was, therefore, negligent and liable for damages.

The *Maci* case was brought before a Wisconsin court. Earlier, in 1976, the Wisconsin Supreme Court found that the duty of care would not be breached if the dangerous condition (that caused the injury) were open and obvious. Negligence would, however, be found if the possessor of the property should have anticipated the harm despite such openness or presumed knowledge. Thus, even though Maci knew or should have known about the dangerous condition, the court concluded that the landlord should have anticipated this harm.

You are a clerk for a Wisconsin Supreme Court justice. Write the section of the majority opinion that distinguishes *Maci* from *Pagelsdorf v. Safeco*.

Your Answer

_____

_____

_____

_____

_____

_____

_____

_____

_____

_____

_____

_____

_____

Model Answer

The court in *Maci* presumes the existence of a duty of care while in *Pagelsdorf,* the issue before the court is whether such a duty exists at all.

In *Maci,* there was a landlord–tenant relationship from which flowed certain legal obligations, including the landlord's obligation or duty to maintain a safe premises. The court in *Pagelsdorf* had to determine whether creating such an obligation between a landlord and a non-tenant guest, and thereby extending the duty of care, was warranted.

Pagelsdorf can also be distinguished from *Maci* because unlike *Maci,* which involved an open, obvious danger, the danger in *Pagelsdorf* was concealed inside of the railing. Thus, instead of serving as a precedent, *Pagelsdorf* establishes a different standard of care, which sets a parameter of negligence opposite that in the Maci case. The court in *Pagelsdorf* attached an arguably more stringent duty of care requiring the landlord to cure hidden defects while in *Maci,* the duty of care concerned protection against open and obvious dangers.

The two cases deal with different standards for applying the duty of care depending upon to whom that duty was owed. *Pagelsdorf* calls for a more rigid test extending the duty beyond existing formal legal obligations while *Maci* does not. Consequently, the two cases can be most effectively used to illustrate the different standards of negligence and duty of care depending upon the relationship of the parties, i.e. landlord/tenant *(Maci)* or landlord/non-tenant guest *(Pagelsdorf)* rather than as controlling precedent.

Constitutional Law

1.) Reread the brief for *Zablocki v. Redhail.*
2.) Read the summary provided for *Moe v. Dinkins.*
3.) Follow the instructions at the end of the case summary.

Case Summary

Moe
v.
Dinkins, 533 F. Supp 623 (1981)

The plaintiffs, both minors living in New York State, wish to marry. Under Section 15 of New York State law, minors cannot marry without first obtaining the written consent of both parents of "the minor or minors or such as shall be living...." Also under Section 15, a female minor between the ages of fourteen and sixteen must obtain judicial approval in addition to the parents' consent. The male and female minors have a child together and wish to marry to "cement their family unit and [to] remove the stigma of illegitimacy from their son...."

The minors have filed a motion for summary judgment claiming that it is unconstitutional and seek to enjoin (prohibit) its enforcement.

The court denied the motion and upheld the statute, claiming that it did not violate the couple's constitutional rights as guaranteed by the Due Process Clause of the Fourteenth Amendment, and that the state interests promoted by the statute were sufficient to tolerate an infringement on the minors' right to marry. The state's interests were deemed to be the protection of minors from immature decision-making and the prevention of unstable marriages. Moreover, the state was deemed to have a valid interest in protecting and promoting "the welfare of children that lack the capacity to act in their own best interests."

These state interests are legitimized under the *parens patriae* power (the states parental role and authority). This position was supported by *Bellotti v. Baird,* in which the U.S. Supreme Court concluded that, "minors often lack the experience, perspective, and judgment necessary to make important, affirmative choices with potentially serious consequences."

When a law allegedly infringes an individuals constitutional right, courts will examine whether the interference, if found to exist, is acceptable given the state interest advanced by the law. To determine this, courts will apply two tests to determine the constitutionality of a law: (1) strict scrutiny and (2) rational relation. Generally, the nature and fundamental importance of the constitutional right at issue determines which test should be used. Under a strict scrutiny test, the court must determine whether there exists a "compelling state interest and whether the statute has been closely tailored to achieve that state interest."

Under the less stringent rational relation test, the court determines whether there is a "rational relation between the means chosen by the state to advance the interest and the legitimate state interest itself." Basically, a court will review whether the state has enacted a statute that accomplishes the stated purpose without overly infringing on an individuals constitutional rights. In *Moe v. Dinkins,* the court had to determine what standard to apply to test whether Section 15 of the New York State law was an unconstitutional violation of an individuals right to marry. It concluded that the rational relation test, rather than the strict scrutiny test, was more appropriate.

In so doing, summary judgment was denied, and the validity of the statute was upheld. The court concluded that the plaintiffs were required to obtain the prior consent of their parents, regardless of whether they wanted to "cement their family unit." The state interest was deemed sufficient to allow this infringement; minors were not prohibited from marrying, they just need their parents' consent. Even if that consent were withheld, the children could presumably wait until majority to marry. Thus, the law was viewed as only an acceptable infringement, not a complete denial of a constitutional right.

Conversely in *Zablocki v. Redhail,* the Wisconsin Supreme Court struck down a state statute requiring parents paying child support and wishing to remarry to first prove that they are current with their payments and that the children are not likely to become wards of the state. In affirming the District Court decision, the Supreme Court held that the right to marry is of fundamental importance...and that "critical examination of the state interests advanced...is required." Upon such an examination, the Supreme Court affirmed the lower court decision that the law unconstitutionally interfered with the fundamental right to marry and was thus unconstitutional.

The strict scrutiny test used by the Supreme Court in *Zablocki* differs from the rational relation test applied in *Moe v. Dinkins*. Although on their face, the two cases appear to be analogous and the courts' reasoning would appear to be inconsistent, the two cases can be distinguished.

You are writing your essay for your law school law review competition. In that essay, you are required to explain how the court in *Moe* could reasonably apply the rational relation test while the court in *Zablocki* could apply the strict scrutiny test.

In addition, you must argue which case you would cite if you were a Supreme Court Justice writing the majority opinion for a decision that upheld a state statute requiring the prior written consent of the guardian(s) of legally retarded adults before they (the retarded adults) are allowed to marry. In your answer, be sure to address which test you would use.

Your Answer

_____

_____

_____

_____

_____

_____

_____

_____

_____

_____

_____

_____

_____

_____

_____

_____

_____

_____

_____

_____

_____

_____

_____

_____

_____

_____

Model Answer

A.) *Moe and Zablocki*

The courts in *Moe v. Dinkins and Zablocki v. Redhail* apply different constitutional tests to determine whether a state statute violates a person's right to marriage. Although both cases dealt with statutes that infringed upon that right, they can be distinguished.

In Moe, the court examined the right of minors to wed, while *Zablocki* dealt with the right of adults. Due to this dissimilarity in the status of the plaintiffs (minor vs. adult), the courts applied different tests. In *Moe,* the court declined to apply the strict scrutiny test because the right of a state to regulate the conduct and actions of minors with regard to marriage was deemed appropriate or strong enough to justify a tolerable infringement on that right. The state had a recognized right under *parens patriae* to oversee the actions of minors and to protect minors when appropriate and when their assumed inability to reason soundly and to act in a mature fashion is in question.

Thus, although the right to marry is a constitutional right, the court deemed that the need to protect minors was a legitimate state interest and that the requirement of receiving the prior consent of their parents before marrying bore a rational relation to that state interest, i.e., it was not an overbroad infringement of their constitutional rights. In essence, the court held that in certain cases, the constitutional rights of children are less inalienable than those of adults. In so ruling, a less stringent standard is warranted and more interference or infringement is tolerated.

In *Zablocki,* the Supreme Court applied the strict scrutiny test. Unlike the rational relation test—which requires the court to find that (1) the states interest being advanced by the statute is valid and (2) that the statute, in advancing that interest, is not overbroad and does not infringe on other interests—the strict scrutiny test is more stringent.

In applying the strict scrutiny test to fundamental constitutional rights, the court must determine that the state has a compelling interest and that the statute is closely tailored to meet that interest. If the court finds that the interest is not compelling or that the statute does not strictly advance that interest, the statute in question will most likely be deemed unconstitutional. In *Zablocki,* the court made such a finding.

Unlike situations involving children, the state cannot interfere with the fundamental right of adults to marry unless the interest in doing so is compelling. According to the Supreme Court, ensuring that child support payments are up to date and that the child will not become a ward of the state are not compelling reasons. In considering the constitutional right of children and adults to marry, and the test to apply, the courts acknowledged that the right differs depending upon the status of the individual. The rights of minors can be infringed upon requiring only a rational basis for doing so, while infringement on an adult's right to marry must be justified by a compelling state interest and the infringement must be closely tailored to meet that interest to withstand strict scrutiny.

B.) Marriage of legally retarded individuals

Before me is a case in which two legally retarded adults wish to marry. Preventing them from doing so, however, is a state statute that requires that before a valid marriage can occur, the retarded adult or adults must obtain the written consent of their guardian or guardians. This court has upheld the statute against a constitutional challenge. In writing the majority opinion, I cite as controlling precedent *Moe v. Dinkins.*

In *Moe v. Dinkins,* the court upheld a New York statute that required minors to receive written consent from their parents before marrying. In its decision, the court cited the need of the state to promote the welfare of children. Within its legitimate powers of *parens patriae,* the state can pass laws that regulate minors marrying.

Additional reasons for the court's decision were that children are often incapable of making sound, reasoned decisions and that children lack the "maturity, experience, and perspective" to make informed and important decisions. Given the nature of the right to marry with respect to children, the court in *Moe* found that a rational relation test was more appropriate than a strict scrutiny test. Accordingly, (1) the state had a legitimate interest in protecting children and (2) that the infringement on their constitutional right to marry of requiring parental consent bore a rational relation to the state interest.

This court has also found that a similar state statute regulating marriage between retarded adults is not unconstitutional. Like minors, many retarded individuals lack the requisite maturity, knowledge, or ability to make informed decisions on a matter as important as marriage. Just as the state has a paternalistic obligation to protect minors from certain actions, that same *parens patriae* power extends to retarded individuals who, in many cases, may chronologically be of majority but who mentally are akin to children or minors. The states interest to prevent uninformed, ill-advised decisions regarding marriage is legitimate and extends to retarded adults.

As in *Moe,* the appropriate standard to determine the constitutionality of the statute is the rational relation test. Does the state have a legitimate interest to protect and does the statute have a rational relation to the interest being advanced?

In this case, yes. The state statute does meet this standard and the state interest is valid. Thus, citing *Moe v. Dinkins* as precedent, we uphold the state law requiring retarded adults to obtain permission from their guardians to marry.

8 | THE ANATOMY OF A CRIME: THE LAW

This section includes a description and explanation of various principles of criminal law, as well as an outline of the elements of some selected crimes that may or may not have been committed in the following fact pattern. At the end, your task is to match the crimes to the fact pattern and answer the questions in a manner that coherently outlines the issues and the crimes involved.

The Elements

Every crime consists of elements, much as a recipe is made of ingredients or an algebra equation consists of variables. And as you probably know, if you forget to add an ingredient like flour when baking a cake, what you have at the end is not cake. Similarly, unless you prepare for every variable in an equation, you cannot solve the problem.

In the law, you have to be equally meticulous in determining whether every element is present to constitute a crime. Therefore, it is necessary to undergo a two-step process to: (1) identify the possible crime and (2) determine whether all of the elements are present to constitute a crime.

To do this, you must be thoroughly familiar with the elements that make up a crime.

In general, every crime must contain the following elements:

ACT (or unlawful omission—the crime results from a failure to act when required to do so by law, such as failing to pay taxes)

INTENT (or *mens rea*)

The act and intent must occur concurrently. This combination of elements is necessary to distinguish between a crime, an accident, and a fortuitous event. If a person inadvertently causes harm, there is no concurrence of act and intent, and quite possibly no crime. Concurrence exists if the act reflects the intent at that same moment.

CAUSATION (the result or outcome of the intentional act)

A useful acronym to remember this simple trio is A.I.C., or to remember it easier, flip it to create C.I.A. Other elements may also be involved, but generally these are the three found in most crimes.

Let's discuss each one. Assume you must determine whether someone who shot a person, who then later died, has committed a crime. First, to commit a crime, there must be an act. The person must have shot the victim (the shooting is the act) or taken some other action.

Next, consider intent or *mens rea*. Intent can be in different degrees. Although intent is perhaps the most complex aspect of criminal law, a simple rule of thumb for our purpose is to ask, "Did the person intend to commit the act with a specific purpose or objective in mind?" If the answer is yes, then we have established intent. If not, there may still be intent, but it may be for a lesser offense. Be aware that some crimes do not require intent (such as parking a car in a prohibited area) and others presume intent from the conduct (such as possession of illegal narcotics).

Causation is essentially the result of the act and the intent. Ask whether the result was due to the defendant's act itself or from some other unrelated force or event. In other words, if not for the defendants act, would the result have occurred? Also, the harm cannot be a remote and indirect consequence that a reasonable person could not have foreseen. If the result, or in this case the crime, came about because of the act and was reasonably foreseeable, we have established causation.

For example, if a person intentionally throws a rock at someone, but the intended target is hit by something other than the rock, the target may, in fact, suffer an injury. The one who threw the rock, however, is not liable for that injury since there is no causation—the injury did not result from the thrown rock. The person may be guilty of assault, if the elements exist, but not necessarily of the injury sustained by the falling object.

Thus, just to review what we have gone over, for each crime that you spot in a fact pattern, you must ask:

(1) Was there an act?

(2) Did the person intend to act in that manner?

(3) Did the act bring about the result or injury?

Then, you must determine whether additional elements for specific crimes are also present. If every necessary element or ingredient is present, then you have established the existence of the crime in question. If the required elements are not present, the accused person is not guilty of that crime. Does this mean, however, that the person is entirely innocent? Certainly not! That person may be guilty of a lesser offense or an "attempt."

An attempt is an incomplete crime or a crime for which all the elements are not satisfied. This notion is easily illustrated through our cake example. Again, if you forget to add flour to the recipe, you do not have a cake, although you *attempted* to bake one. The same is true in the law. If a person shoots another, but the victim does not die, the assailant cannot be guilty of murder; rather he or she may be guilty of "attempted" murder.

Now that we have done our initial review of the basic elements of a crime, let's discuss the specific crimes.

The Crimes

The law is essentially logical; however, problems can arise in its application to a specific set of facts. Thus, to identify the crimes in the facts, remember one simple tip: if something strikes you as illegal, it probably is. Also, be aware that every crime has possible defenses. For this exercise, however, focus solely on identifying the crimes rather than on proffering possible defenses.

Crimes will vary to some extent from state to state. In some jurisdictions, crimes are codified in a criminal code. In others, common law, i.e., judge-made law through precedent still governs. Nonetheless, crimes can generally be broken down into three basic categories:

(1) Homicides

(2) Non-homicidal crimes against the person

(3) Crimes against property

Other categories not discussed here include crimes against public morality—such as prostitution—and crimes against the state—such as treason, sedition, and contempt.

Homicides involve a death; non-homicides are crimes against a person that do not result in death; and, as the name implies, crimes against property are just that. In addition, we will also discuss other crimes such as conspiracy and the felony murder doctrine, which are major topics in any law school criminal law curriculum.

1. Homicides typically include:

Murder

Manslaughter

Murder is the intentional killing of another without legal justi-fication. Manslaughter is the killing of another where there is some intervening cause or provocation immediately prior to the killing that mitigates the killer's intent. That is, manslaughter could be a killing done in the heat of passion. Finding one's spouse engaged in improper behavior with another and suddenly lunging at the suitor's throat with a knife, thereby killing him or her, has been found by courts to be a sufficient intervening force or provocation to consti-tute murder in the heat of passion, or manslaughter.

You should note that a person could be guilty of murder if he or she did not intend to kill the victim, but due to their conduct, a homicide was likely to occur. That is, if you act in a manner evidenc-ing a wanton and willful disregard for human life, but do not intend to kill a person, yet they die, you can be found guilty of murder. An unintentional killing resulting from a reckless act can, therefore, constitute murder.

There is also voluntary and involuntary manslaughter. Voluntary manslaughter is similar to the heat of passion example. The crime would be considered murder if there had not been an adequate intervening cause or provocation. The key here is that the actor's state of mind (*mens rea*) is neither wicked nor malicious. To estab-lish voluntary manslaughter as an exception to murder, you must prove: (1) adequate provocation; (2) producing passion and an act; (3) resulting in death; (4) without an adequate cooling-off or rest period between the provocation and the killing.

Involuntary manslaughter is an unintentional homicide. It is often due to reckless behavior that results in death. Driving a car while intoxicated and then killing a pedestrian crossing a street would constitute involuntary manslaughter.

2. Non-homicidal crimes against the person typically include:

a. Battery

b. Assault

  b. Kidnapping

  c. False imprisonment

Not every crime results in death. A beating can be a crime even though the victim or victims survive. Brandishing a weapon at another can also be a crime, even if the weapon is not discharged or even loaded. The beating, or battery, can be considered a crime if the elements or ingredients exist. The same is true for assault that may or may not have been committed by the brandishing of the weapon.

3.　Crimes against property typically include:

  a. Robbery

  b. Burglary

  c. Larceny

  d. Embezzlement

  e. False pretenses

  f. Forgery

  g. Receipt of stolen goods

  h. Extortion

Unfortunately, today we are all too aware of the many crimes that are perpetrated against property. If someone takes your coat without your permission, that is a crime. If someone breaks into your house to steal something, it is a crime. The list goes on. What is important to remember is that like a homicide or another crime against the person, every element that constitutes a crime against property must also be present to have a crime, or at the least, an attempted crime.

Following are the general elements of some key crimes.

Homicides

Murder

To establish murder as a crime, there must be: (1) an act; (2)an intent—the perpetrator must have intended to act with the objective of killing the person, usually a deliberate, pre-meditated intent; (3) concurrence of the act and intent and; (4) causation—the death must have been caused by the act.

Manslaughter

Like murder, there must have been an act, but the requisite intent is less than that for murder because there was an adequate provocation or intervening cause immediately preceding the killing.

Voluntary manslaughter—adequate, sudden provocation

Involuntary manslaughter—criminal negligence or extreme recklessness substitutes for the intent

To establish causation, it is necessary to prove that the provoked or sudden act caused the death.

Non-Homicidal Crimes Against the Person

Battery

Battery is the unlawful touching of another, resulting in offensive touching or bodily injury. There must be an act—touching—and causation—touching must cause the injury. The touching must also be unlawful, that is, without consent and rather than causing an injury, it may be offensive. Battery is one of the few crimes where state of mind can be unimportant, i.e., intent is not required. A defendant can be guilty of battery if he unlawfully touches another, causing injury with criminal negligence. A trick question often seen on law school exams asks whether an adult who suddenly, and intentionally, grabs a cane from a person's hand is guilty of a battery. At no time did the adult physically touch the victim's person.

The answer is *yes;* battery was committed. You should note that a person does not have to physically touch another in order for there to be battery. All a person has to do is offensively and intentionally touch a person—an object considered a part or an extension of that person: i.e., a cane or even a plate the person is holding that someone snatches from their hand.

Assault

An assault is an attempted battery or conduct intentionally placing a person in reasonable apprehension that imminent bodily harm will occur. If you brandish a gun at a person who, as a result, is deathly afraid, you have committed an assault. This is true even if the gun was not loaded or if the gun was a toy. All that matters is the person reasonably believed the gun to be loaded and/or real.

Thus, the act is the placing of the person in reasonable apprehension, the intent is your desire to make that person apprehensive, and the causation is the result. If the person knows that the gun is only a water pistol, you cannot have an assault because any apprehension would most likely be unreasonable.

In general, when you spot what you think is a crime, simply see if all of the ingredients or elements that make an event a crime actually exist. If you do this and do it correctly, you are on your way toward thinking like a lawyer and finding out whether you have the aptitude and, indeed, the interest for the law.

Kidnapping

Well, we think you all can recognize a kidnapping when you see it, or can you? You may never have realized that there really are elements to a kidnapping. For an act to be considered a kidnapping, you must, once again, have an act to confine a person against his or her will, by force or threat of force, or by deceit or fraud; the intent, as well as some new elements—movement of the victim and con-cealment. One could consider this element causation just to make our acronym stick—the confinement is the result of the intentional act, and the confinement must be against the victim's will.

False Imprisonment

Like kidnapping, false imprisonment is also a crime against a person and involves the usual act, intent, and causation. Generally, false imprisonment is the intentional confinement of a person against his or her will. If the victim has a reasonable way of escaping, you do not have false imprisonment. The act is the intentional confinement of a person, the intent is the desire to confine a person, and causation is the resulting confinement. False imprisonment generally differs from kidnapping in that it does not involve concealment of the person.

Crimes Against Property

Robbery

"Stop! I've been robbed!" is a cry heard all too often these days. To have a crime of robbery, there must be an act, intent, and causation. There must also be (1) an unlawful taking (2) of the personal property of another (3) by force or by the threat of an immediate use of force.

Thus, for example, if you are walking down the street and someone runs up to you and snatches your gold chain, watch, or purse, a robbery has been committed. There was an unlawful act (the snatching), the act was intentional (the robber intended to take the chain), and the chain was snatched from your neck (force was used).

Since all the elements of the crime of robbery existed, the person was indeed guilty of the crime.

Burglary

Modern statutes generally describe burglary as: (1) the unlawful breaking and entering of a dwelling (2) of another and (3) with the intent to commit a crime therein. Thus, in the situation where someone entered another's house by opening a window to steal a stereo, he has committed a burglary. Note that the element of "breaking" does not require an actual breaking of, say, a door or other object to gain entry, a simple entry is sufficient.

Larceny

Larceny is: (1) an unlawful taking or the gaining of control of and carrying away (2) the personal property of another (3) with the intent to permanently deprive them of that property. In common, everyday parlance, stealing. Larceny differs from robbery in that larceny lacks the use of force.

Taking a piece of gum from a candy store is larceny. You take the gum intentionally, it is not yours since you did not buy it. Once you start chewing it, you certainly do not plan to return it to its original owner. Become familiar with this crime and its elements as you will need to recognize it.

Embezzlement

Embezzlement is what takes place everyday on Wall Street, end of lesson. Well, maybe it's not quite that simple. Embezzlement is (1) the fraudulent or unauthorized (2) intentional appropriation or seizing of the (3) personal property of (4) another (5) while having lawful possession of that property.

If someone gives you money to pay a bill for them, but instead you keep the money, you have committed embezzlement.

By applying the elements to those facts (there was fraud, there was an intentional seizing of the personal property of another, and you were in lawful possession of the money—they gave it to you willingly) we can conclude that the crime was committed.

False Pretenses

False pretenses means (1) obtaining title (2) to the personal property of another by (3) an intentional misrepresentation with (4) the desire to defraud. All the elements of this crime must be present to find a person guilty of false pretenses. For the purposes of our exercise, we will not elaborate further on the different permutations of false pretenses.

Forgery

This is why we no longer simply place an "X" on the line requiring our signature. To be convicted as a forger, you must (1) act with the intent to defraud by (2) writing that (3) falsely misrepresents another. There are technicalities concerning whether a third person was fraudulently induced to sign a document, but again, this is not necessary for our purposes.

Receipt of Stolen Goods

This is another crime in the wild, crazy world of criminal activity. To be convicted of receiving stolen property, one must receive property (2) that you know was obtained illegally by another person, but still you take it with (3) the intent to deprive the rightful owner of the property.

You're walking down the street and you see someone climbing out of a broken window with a new stereo. Instead of alerting the authorities, you say to yourself, "Hey, I was looking for a stereo just like that." You rush to the person who has just jumped to the sidewalk from the window and you ask, "Attention shopper, how would you like fifty dollars for that stereo?" By the way, the burglar alarm is ringing.

You give the fellow a fifty and then you run off with your stereo, take it home, plug it in, and invite your friends over for a party. Now tell us, are you guilty of receiving stolen property? Let's just say you can write and tell us all about it once you're comfortably settled in at Attica.

Extortion

Extortion is a bully crime. When someone who can cause you great personal or physical harm demands payment or property for not harming you, that person is an extortionist and you are being extorted.

The elements are (1) obtaining property from another (2) by wrongful use or threat of force or coercion.

Conspiracy

To have a conspiracy, you must find that two or more people worked in concert to accomplish an illegal objective or a legal objective by illegal means. It does not matter if the illegal objective or the illegal means to complete an act are unsuccessful. The elements of a conspiracy are (1) an intentional agreement (2) by two or more persons (3) to commit the illegal objective or to do the illegal acts. In some jurisdictions, there is also the requirement that an act be committed that furthers the conspiracy, referred to as an "overt act."

Criminal Trespass

Trespass is the (1) intentional (2) invasion of (3) one's property without the owner's permission. Examples of a trespass are easy. Anytime you have taken a shortcut across someones lawn, you have trespassed. However, trespassing need not involve property such as a yard or field. Any restricted area intentionally invaded without permission may constitute a trespass.

Felony Murder

The felony murder doctrine is a major aspect of any first year criminal law course. Under this doctrine or rule, a defendant can be found guilty of any death that occurs during the commission of a felony as long as that death was a foreseeable result of the act. In other words, the felony must have been the proximate cause or the reason for the death. Still another way of looking at it is that the death was part of a logical chain of events that resulted from the criminal activity.

Thus, to establish felony murder, you must have (1) the intent to commit a felony, (2) a death caused during the commission of the felony, and (3) the death must be related to the felony by an unbroken chain of events.

For example, if party "A" robs a bank, holds several patrons hostage, and one of the hostages dies of a heart attack during the incident, party "A" is guilty of at least an attempted robbery and guilty for the death of the hostage as well.

As a law student, you would argue that but for the robbery or attempted robbery, the hostage would likely not have suffered a fatal heart attack. In many instances, key to determining guilt under the felony murder doctrine is whether the death that occurred was in fact foreseeable.

The felony murder doctrine would also apply if the hostage was shot by the robber's accomplice. If the hostage dies because of that wound, both felons would be guilty of murder under the doctrine. The death would have occurred as part of the direct chain of events stemming from the robbery, or the underlying felony. It sounds complicated, but it is not. Again, when in doubt, fall back on your analysis of each of the elements.

Remember that, in law, there is rarely only one right answer. The key is to make a persuasive, logical argument about why your answer is acceptable and you will probably get some credit.

Solicitation

Solicitation is (1) the intentional urging of (2) another to (3) commit a crime. It does not matter if the person actually committed the crime. You are guilty merely because you urged him or her to commit the crime. If you encourage a friend to use fake identification to buy beer because they are under age, but they refuse, you are guilty of solicitation, even though they did not carry out your wishes.

Mayhem

Historically, mayhem was the intentional dismemberment of another or the disablement of a bodily part. Under modern statutes, mayhem also includes permanent disfigurement that does not involve the removal or dismemberment of a bodily part. Some states require a specific intent to maim or disfigure; others have abolished the crime of mayhem and instead consider the crime to be an aggravated battery.

Rape

Rape is unlawful sexual intercourse with a woman by a man who is not her husband. At common law, a rape has not occurred if:

(1) A woman forces intercourse on a man

(2) The parties are of the same sex

(3) The parties are husband and wife

Also, at common law, sexual intercourse is defined as penetration of the female sex organ by the male sex organ. Several states have codified statutes altering the common law conception of rape to allow a husband to be prosecuted for the rape of his wife. Finally, effective consent by the woman will discharge a suspect from liability for rape, except, of course, with respect to victims under the legal age of consent, or if consent is improperly obtained, for example, by fraud, threats, or force.

In summary, the above crimes represent some of those that may or may not be present in the fact pattern. It is your job to take this information and apply it to the following story. Then, answer the questions provided. Bear in mind that these questions reflect the types of questions on a law school exam.

Each question asks you to identify the crimes; when answering, remember to first spot what you think is a crime and then analyze whether the necessary elements are present. Keep the acronym A.I.C. or C.I.A. in mind, and determine whether additional elements need to be present for each crime as well. If you become adept in approaching and analyzing legal problems in this manner, you will be well on your way to a successful law school career. Good luck!

9 | THE ANATOMY OF A CRIME: THE PROBLEM

Your Assignment

Now that you've graduated from the *So, You Want to be a Lawyer* School of Law, it's time to get a job. So today you are a junior attorney in the Massachusetts District Attorney's office. Your first assignment, should you decide to accept it or be fired, is to read the following compilation of testimony given by four college students and a number of others who are witnesses in a case being investigated by the D.A.'s office.

Your task is simple: review the facts as recited by the witnesses and answer the questions following the facts. Remember, when reading the facts, think about the law that you reviewed in the previous section and how it can apply to the facts. To answer the questions, you will need a thorough understanding of both the law and the facts as presented below. Take as much time as you need to read the facts.

While answering the questions, revisit the law section as much as you need. Some of the questions have suggested time limits; when possible try to adhere to these limits as this will provide a more accurate feel for what it's like to take a law school exam. Good luck!

The Fact Pattern

Harvard University, Cambridge, Massachusetts

Music of the high mass fills the air. Bronze statutes perch high on ivy-covered buildings, icons of power and prestige. Harvard University, where the best and the brightest assemble to compete, achieve, divide, and conquer.

A glance through a large stained-glass window into the massive gothic structure provides a view of a well-appointed rehearsal room. The intense notes of a classical piano solo grow louder and clearer. Spotlights accentuate large oil paintings in gold leaf antique frames; portraits of Harvard graduates from a bygone era.

A shimmer of moonlight falls onto the hands traversing black and white keys.

At eighteen, MILES is braving a new world of privilege and comfort, far from his working class roots. Careful and kind, with good looks and charm, he yearns for acceptance.

He stumbles as he plays; then stops and curses. Out of the background emerges Charlotte, nineteen, with a look of innocence and girlish charm.

CHARLOTTE – You're still practicing?

Surprised by Charlotte, Miles hits his head on the lamp over the sheet music.

MILES – OW!

CHARLOTTE - Are you all right?

MILES – Yeah, but I won't be if I don't get this fellowship.

CHARLOTTE – So you decided to apply for a Steinmann?

MILES – I have to, my financial aid isn't enough to cover everything.

Charlotte walks over to him and kisses him tenderly on the cheek.

CHARLOTTE – I'm sure you'll do great!

MILES – I hope so.

Charlotte smiles.

CHARLOTTE – I'm going over to J.P.'s. Do you want to come?

MILES – No. I think I should stay here a little longer. Maybe later.

CHARLOTTE – Okay, but don't work too hard.

Miles tousles Charlotte's hair affectionately as she reluctantly kisses him goodbye.

Harvard Square convenience store—immediately following.

Nathan, twenty-one years old, has black hair and piercing eyes that miss nothing. He wanders down the aisle, grabbing a six-pack of beer, when he sees Miles ahead of him.

NATHAN – Miles . . . Hi, I'm Nathan Scott, Charlotte's friend.

MILES – Oh hi, I remember. You just transferred from . . .

NATHAN – The Sorbonne.

MILES – That's right . . .

Nathan sets down the beer and shakes Miles's hand.

NATHAN – How's freshman year treating you?

Miles follows Nathan as he continues to talk and walk down the aisle, stuffing bags of chips and dip in his basket.

MILES – It beats the steel mills back home.

They arrive at the cash register where Nathan puts his things down.

Miles puts his things behind Nathan's. The clerk totals Nathan's purchases. Nathan looks at Miles's things.

NATHAN – Let me get that for you.

Nathan pulls out his wallet.

NATHAN – (to the store clerk) It's all together.

MILES – No, really, I've got it.

Nathan looks at Miles skeptically as Miles hands a crumpled dollar bill and a fistful of change to the clerk.

NATHAN – So where're you headed?

MILES – Back to the dorm.

NATHAN – A bunch of us are hanging out, why don't you come over?

MILES – I don't know, I wanted to get an early jump on my classes.

NATHAN – You've got to be kidding, classes just started last week.

MILES – I know but . . .

NATHAN – Take it from an upperclassman, you study long, you study wrong.

Miles smiles.

J.P. and Nathan's apartment later that night.

J.P. is twenty and a senior; his long red ponytail gives him the air of nineties counter-culture as he lounges in front of the TV with a bottle of beer in his hand. The stereo blares in the background as the group stares at a silent television.

Summer emerges from the kitchen with a plate of pizza. Voluptuous and stylish, her shiny blonde hair perfectly suits her mischievous air. Miles sits on the couch while Charlotte sits between his legs on the floor.

SUMMER – J.P., turn up the TV; my brother was in that kid's class.

The group turns to the television where we see Melody Maxwell.

TELEVISION REPORTER – This is Melody Maxwell from Action 9 News, and I'm here at Newman Prep with Rusty Thurman.

We see the reporter hold the microphone up to a teenage boy in a wheelchair.

REPORTER – We're here on the anniversary of a tragic car accident that left Rusty paralyzed. But today, one year later, Rusty has been named class president and has been accepted to MIT.

The reporter turns to Rusty.

REPORTER – Rusty, it must take a lot of courage to come back the way you did. Were you ever afraid that you wouldn't be able to have the kind of life you had before the accident?

Rusty smiles, but shakes his head firmly no.

RUSTY – For a while I didn't know what to think, but with the help of my friends, I was able to realize that the only thing that was really holding me back were my fears, and once I was able to put them in perspective and confront them, I came to learn that nothing could get in my way.

J.P. shakes his head sadly.

J.P. – Dang, that's deep.

REPORTER – Well, Rusty you're an inspiration to us all.

Summer turns the TV down again.

SUMMER – That kid's got a lot of courage.

CHARLOTTE – Really.

J.P. – It kinda makes you wonder where he got it from. You can't learn that in school.

NATHAN – That's not true. Last year at the Sorbonne we studied a group that helped each other overcome their fears by confronting them.

J.P. – You're kidding.

NATHAN – No. I mean, not overcoming your fears is the single greatest impediment to personal achievement.

J.P. – Where'd you read that?

NATHAN – My father did an article on it in the *New England Journal of Medicine*. He surveyed more than a thousand men and women as to what was the single factor that prohibited them from living a full life. Eight-five percent of the respondents said it was their fears.

SUMMER – So what does all that mean?

NATHAN – Well, he concluded that the only way to live a full life was to overcome your fears.

J.P. – I guess in theory it makes sense.

NATHAN – And as a practical matter, the key thing is to confront them before you're forced to, like the kid in the news story.

MILES – Right, but who actually takes the time to confront their fears?

NATHAN – A lot of people do. Like I said, we studied numerous cases of people who did. It's not such a bad idea.

CHARLOTTE – Well I hope you aren't suggesting anything like that now!

NATHAN – Why not? Freud said that refusing to confront your fears was a classic sign of mental illness.

SUMMER – If anything, it's counter-intuitive.

NATHAN – Listen, I'm talking about taking a clinically proven approach to overcoming our fears.

Nathan looks around the room.

NATHAN – I'm sure we all have some deep-rooted fear or phobia that we'd rather not have.

J.P. – And?

NATHAN – And we could help each other get over it. All we have to do is put our name and fear on individual pieces of paper and pull lots. Whomever you get is the one you help.

SUMMER – So no one knows who've you selected?

NATHAN – Of course not. There has to be an element of surprise for it to work.

Summer looks at Nathan skeptically.

MILES – Did everybody in that group get over their fears?

Nathan walks over to the desk and takes out a pad and pen.

NATHAN – Just about.

CHARLOTTE – Come on, Nathan, this may do more harm than good.

SUMMER – She's right. Curiosity killed the cat.

Nathan writes his name and fear on a piece of paper.

NATHAN – But satisfaction brought him back.

MILES – I don't know if I'm into this.

NATHAN – Why not?

MILES – It sounds too risky.

NATHAN – Look, we all just watched that young kid say how he had to confront his fears to overcome being paralyzed, and here we are in perfect health. And you're saying you don't want to make an effort to perhaps improve the quality of your life. Besides, I'm not talking about some stupid frat prank.

A pregnant pause.

J.P. – I'll do it, if everybody else does.

J.P. writes his name and fear on the paper. He starts to pass it to Charlotte, but Nathan takes the pad and pen and gives it to Miles instead.

NATHAN – Charlotte, you shouldn't do it if you're not comfortable with it.

Charlotte smiles gratefully.

CHARLOTTE – Thanks, I think I'll pass.

NATHAN – C'mon Miles, you came to Harvard because you wanted a challenge, right?

J.P. (to Miles) – C'mon. You gotta believe to belong.

Miles hesitates and then reluctantly takes the pad and writes his name and fear on a piece of paper, folds it, and puts the paper in the pile. Miles then passes the pen and pad to Summer and she does the same. Nathan picks up the slips of paper and begins to read.

NATHAN – Miles, claustrophobia. Summer, falling. J.P., paralysis. And Nathan, death.

Nathan pauses after reading the names and fears, the mood in the room is serious and quiet. Summer turns to J.P.

SUMMER – Why are you afraid of being paralyzed?

J.P. – 'Cause of my ole man. Thanks to the Vietnam War, I've never seen him walk.

There is silence until Summer clears her throat.

SUMMER – Well, I have to be honest. My shrink said I've never gotten over my mom walking out on my dad and that's why I have this fear of falling.

CHARLOTTE – Did he say how you could get over it?

SUMMER – Not really, I stopped going to therapy.

Summer drains her wine glass slowly.

SUMMER – What about you, Miles?

MILES – Well, I'm claustrophobic. I guess it's because I got locked in an abandoned refrigerator when I was a kid.

J.P. – That's a bummer.

MILES – Yeah.

NATHAN – So whenever you feel trapped, you have a panic attack?

MILES – Something like that.

SUMMER – How'd you get out?

MILES – My buddy found me.

J.P. – How about you, Nathan?

NATHAN – Death. What else is there?

SUMMER – So why are you afraid of death?

NATHAN – 'Cause we don't know what's out there.

SUMMER – Well, don't you believe in God?

NATHAN – What's that got to do with it?

SUMMER – Everything. Fear of the unknown is a way of doubting God.

NATHAN – Oh, please.

Nathan carefully refolds each piece of paper, puts them in a bowl, and has each person pick a name.

NATHAN – For this to work no one can say anything to anybody. Agreed?

Everyone nods affirmatively.

Auditorium-style classroom—the next day.

J.P. is being grilled by their engineering professor, a British gentleman who is lecturing from a slide on an overhead projector.

PROFESSOR – Mr. Michaels, do you care to tell the class what the study of kinetics is all about?

J.P. – Right now?

The class laughs.

PROFESSOR – If you want to increase your odds of passing this course, I'd suggest that you do it immediately.

J.P. nonchalantly flips through his textbook and looks up at the professor calmly.

J.P. – Well, since you put it that way, I'd say that kinetics is the study of the relation between asymmetric forces and the changes in motion that result.

PROFESSOR – So how is that notion best illustrated?

J.P. smirks confidently.

J.P. – I'd say that the gravitational free fall formula is perhaps the best illustration.

The professor points to a formula on the screen.

PROFESSOR – That's correct.

Miles, who is running late, slips in through the back door and sits next to J.P. Without turning around, the professor glances at his seating chart and calls on Miles.

PROFESSOR – Mr. Broussard, why don't you tell us which law applies in this instance.

Miles shifts nervously as he tries to get his bearings. J.P. quickly scribbles the answer on a sheet of paper.

MILES – Newton's Second Law.

PROFESSOR – Which states?

J.P. scribbles the answer again.

MILES – Force equals mass times acceleration.

The professor turns back to the class.

PROFESSOR – Well, it seems that you and Mr. Michaels have all the answers today. I hope for your sake that you can keep it up.

A few students snicker.

MILES (whispering to J.P.) – Thanks. That was a close call.

J.P. – Don't worry about it.

Outside the classroom—immediately following.

Miles waves goodbye to J.P. and hurries off to his next class. As J.P. saunters out of the building, engrossed in thought, his watch alarm sounds. He reaches into his pocket and quickly swallows two of his agoraphobia pills. He jumps back startled as Nathan emerges from the shadows.

J.P. – Wow, you scared me!

Nathan smiles as he walks alongside J.P.

NATHAN – Sorry.

J.P. – So what's up?

NATHAN – Not much, I just got out of Biochem.

J.P. – I hear that's a tough one.

NATHAN – Not really, I already covered a lot of the material last year.

J.P. – That's pretty lucky.

NATHAN – Yeah . . . So, have you thought about what we talked about the other night?

J.P. – You mean that whole fear thing?

NATHAN – Yeah.

J.P. – Not really.

NATHAN – Well, maybe we should talk. I've got some ideas.

J.P. looks at him suddenly intrigued.

J.P. – Okay.

Charlotte's art studio–early that same evening.

The haunting strains of Ravel wind through the studio mingling with the sound of the wind.

The room is dimly lit and Miles and Charlotte sit crosslegged on the floor surrounded by half-finished canvases and crumpled tubes of paint. Miles sighs, stretching his legs in front of him contentedly.

MILES – Who's this...? I don't think I've heard it before...

CHARLOTTE – Ravel ... I don't play it much.

MILES – How come?

CHARLOTTE – 'Cause it always makes me a little sad.

Miles draws her nearer to him and strokes her hair gently.

MILES – Don't be sad.

Charlotte smiles shyly as Miles's eyes penetrate hers. He pulls her closer to him and then starts to kiss her hair and then her face. She turns her lips to him, looping her arms around his neck and dropping to the floor as he slowly unbuttons her blouse. Suddenly the door creaks open slowly.

NATHAN – Hi.

Charlotte bolts up in surprise. Miles's eyes meet Nathan's cold stare.

NATHAN– I hope I'm not interrupting anything. I brought you some dinner.

Nathan hands Charlotte a small paper bag.

CHARLOTTE – Uh . . . Thanks.

Embarrassed, Charlotte takes the bag. Miles tries to hide his annoyance as he shakes Nathan's hand.

MILES – What's up?

Quickly getting up and smoothing her skirt, Charlotte walks over to the other side of the room self-consciously and turns off the music.

CHARLOTTE – Nathan, have you seen my other easel?

NATHAN – I put it up there.

Nathan grabs a longpole and slides the trap door open revealing a small dark area. He turns to Miles.

NATHAN – Why don't you get it? I pulled a muscle at the gym.

Miles's cheeks flush red as he looks up at the tiny crawlspace. There's an uncomfortable silence and then Nathan throws up his hands in sudden realization.

NATHAN – Oh Miles, I'm sorry. I forgot you were claustrophobic. Really, I'm sorry.

Nathan takes the pole and slides the door shut. Miles looks at him suspiciously but says nothing as he grabs his books.

MILES – Charlotte, I better run.

CHARLOTTE – You don't have to go.

NATHAN – Really, there's plenty of food.

MILES – No, that's okay. It's almost 8 and I really need to get to the library. But I'll call you later.

CHARLOTTE – Okay.

Charlotte looks visibly disappointed as she puts her arm through Miles's and walks him reluctantly to the door.

Still annoyed at Nathan, but trying not to show it, Miles kisses Charlotte lightly on the cheek. Nathan's eyes follow Miles out the door as he closes it behind him.

NATHAN – You guys have gotten close pretty quickly.

Charlotte looks away blushing.

CHARLOTTE – Yeah, he's really nice.

NATHAN – He seems to be a real gentleman.

Becoming increasingly embarrassed, Charlotte looks away from Nathan's piercing eyes.

CHARLOTTE – Well, yeah. He is.

NATHAN – I hope so.

Nathan starts to unpack the food nonchalantly.

NATHAN – 'Cause I'd hate to see you hurt.

Nathan offers Charlotte a piece of sushi. She shakes her head and stares ahead, troubled.

CHARLOTTE – Well I don't think Miles would do anything like that.

NATHAN – Charlotte, he's a man.

Nathan coolly pops a piece of sushi in his mouth.

J.P.'s bedroom—the next night.

From Nathan's point of view from the hallway outside J.P.'s room, we see J.P. sitting at the computer punching in numbers. J.P. sits anxiously waiting for something to come up on the screen. After a moment, there's a buzz and the screen fills with words and numbers.

J.P. smiles triumphantly as BUILDING SYSTEMS-HARVARD UNIVERSITY comes up on the screen. Still, without J.P. noticing, Nathan looks at the screen and then slips quietly into his own room.

Widener Library—a few days later.

The darkness of winter's approach covers the campus like a gray cloud. Through one of the windows of Widener Library, we enter a dark, cavernous netherworld where the only light comes from thin florescent bulbs arched over desks crammed between the bookcases.

There's silence except for the sounds of dry pages turning. Miles and J.P. sit at a desk with books piled in front of them.

J.P. – You took five classes and Liman for calculus? Are you nuts? That's an upper level course!

MILES – I have to in order to major in music and engineering.

J.P. – Double major! Are you crazy? Nobody double majors at Harvard!

Beads of perspiration break out on Miles's forehead.

J.P. – You're kidding.

Miles looks down nervously.

MILES – No. I wanted to be able to understand engineering principles so that I could apply them to music programs.

J.P. – I hear you.

J.P. pats Miles on the back reassuringly.

J.P. – Well, if you need any help just let me know.

Miles looks at him gratefully as J.P. gathers his things.

J.P. – Have you figured out a scheme yet?

MILES – What are you talking about?

J.P. – Nathan's fear experiment.

MILES – I don't care about Nathan. My only concern is getting through freshman year and winning the Steinmann.

J.P. – Just asking.

Miles looks scared and angry as he pulls out his books.

J.P.'s room—a few nights later.

The apartment is quiet. The door to J.P.'s room slowly opens and Nathan walks in. The room is empty.

Nathan looks around and then walks over to the computer. He punches in numbers. BUILDING SYSTEMS – HARVARD UNIVERSITY comes up on the screen. Nathan begins punching in other numbers. After a moment, we hear a buzz. Nathan punches in something and then turns the computer off. Silently and quickly, he slips back into his room.

A conference room in Peabody Terrace Dormitory—the same night.

As Summer sits on the couch, she absorbs the view from the twentieth floor of Peabody Terrace. There are about a dozen students sitting comfortably at a conference table as an older professor drones on in the background.

Harvard Music Building—the same night.

Miles and Charlotte walk down a narrow hallway toward a large, well-lit room. Miles takes a deep breath as he walks in. A sign says

STEINMANN TRIALS. A large grand piano is in the middle of the room. Other than a committee of professors talking among themselves, the room is empty. Charlotte squeezes Miles's hand and slips into a seat in the back of the room.

J.P.'s bedroom—the same night.
J.P. is hunched over the computer screen. Rolls of documents bearing the seal of the DEPARTMENT OF BUILDINGS AND PERMITS are scattered across the bed.

Music Hall backstage—same time.
In a dimly lit hallway, a technician stands in front of a large row of circuit breakers and switches. He looks at a sheet of paper, double-checking his mission.
Turning back to the board, he hits a switch and a bulb on the piano comes on as Miles patiently waits for his cue. The professors are now quiet.
One of them nods to Miles. Miles looks over at Charlotte who smiles and gives him the thumbs up. Miles starts to play. Slowly, at first, a gentle melody. And then the song turns darker, crashing into the heavy bass keys. As the songpeaks, Miles becomes consumed with the music. And over the sound of his playing we see—

J.P.'s bedroom—the same time.
J.P.'s eyes quickly scan the computer screen. He types in a code and the screen changes color. Now rows of numbers fill the screen. He types in another code and the numbers quickly reconfigure on the screen.

Peabody Terrace hallway—later that night.
Summer closes the apartment door and walks with three friends toward the elevator. They don't notice someone watching them, silhouetted in the shadows.

J.P.'s bedroom—same time.

J.P. picks up the ringing phone. We see the computer screen—HARVARD BUILDING SYSTEMS. J.P. punches in another number and the words PEABODY TERRACE come up on the screen.

Hallway Peabody Terrace—same time.

The person we saw watching Summer whispers into a portable phone. From his point of view, we see Summer and her friends getting in the elevator.

PERSON – She just got on elevator number two with three others.

J.P.'s room—same time.

J.P. hangs up the phone and hurriedly punches numbers into the screen. The words PEABODY TERRACE fill the screen. J.P. types LOCKPROGRAM onto the screen andpresses ENTER.

Hallway Peabody Terrace—same time.

The elevator doors are slowly closing. The professor from the class runs toward the elevator, breathing hard.

PROFESSOR – Hold the elevator!

Inside the elevator—same time.

Summer pushes the DOOR OPEN button. The doors glide open and the professor squeezes in. She smiles at Summer appreciatively and pushes the fifteenth floor.

J.P.'s bedroom – same time.

J.P. answers the ringing phone.

PERSON (O.S.) — Stop the program!

J.P. – What?

PERSON – Stop the program!

J.P. immediately begins punching numbers into the computer. But the words LOCK PROGRAM flash persistently. A look of cold panic creeps across his face.

Inside the elevator—same time.

The elevator is on the twentieth floor. It starts to go down smoothly, passing the eighteenth, seventeenth, and sixteenth floors. The professor moves to the front of the elevator. She looks up at the row of floor numbers. The light goes off on fifteen. The professor presses DOOR OPEN. The doors open slightly and then slam shut. The elevator starts going back up. The floor lights flash sixteen, seventeen, eighteen, nineteen . . .

Basement office—Peabody Terrace—same time.

The building superintendent's eyes are glued to a black and white television. COMPUTER OVERRIDE lights up the board tracking the elevators. Noticing the board, he scrambles to the phone.

SUPERINTENDENT – It's Kovack at Peabody.

He punches the control board clumsily.

SUPERINTENDENT – I've got an override.

J.P.'s bedroom—same time.

J.P. is bent over his computer, banging in numbers, cursing to himself. LOCK PROGRAM still flashes on the screen.

Inside the elevator—same time.

The elevator stops. The twentieth floor is lit. Trembling, Summer walks to the front, pushing DOOR OPEN. Nothing. She pushes it again. Again, nothing. The lights on the board flash, and then stop. Now the elevator starts to fall. Fast. The numbers begin to light up one by one.

Superintendent's office—same time.
The superintendent's breath comes in short wheezes. He's punching buttons seemingly randomly, praying that some combination will work.
SUPERINTENDENT – Come on. . . . Come on!

Inside the elevator—same time.
Summer is kneeling hunched in the corner, pale and anguished. All eyes are glued to the elevator board as the professor and the other women watch the floor lights sixteen, fifteen, fourteen, thirteen, twelve, eleven . . .

Inside the elevator shaft—same time.
The elevator shoots to the bottom of the shaft, creaking with the speed.
J.P.'s bedroom—same time.
J.P. slams his hand against the computer screen angrily. LOCKPROGRAM fills the screen. Suddenly he grabs the cord and yanks it from the outlet.

Inside the elevator shaft—same time.
The elevator rushes toward the floor, shivers, and then stops a few feet from the bottom.

Superintendent's basement office—same time.
The words COMPUTER OVERRIDE flash off. The board goes blank. The superintendent drops into the chair.

J.P.'s room—same time.
J.P. lays his head on his desk. The computer screen is blank. He fumbles for the cord and plugs the computer back in. The words HAVE A NICE DAY flash on.

Inside the elevator—minutes later.
Paramedics swarm the elevator. Summer is unconscious. Her eyes open slowly as a paramedic passes smelling salts under her nose. The other three women are huddled around the professor, who's motionless. An oxygen mask is quickly placed over her face.

Outside Charlotte's parents' summer house—about an hour outside Boston—later that same evening.
Charlotte's car is parked outside her parents' spacious brick summer home, perched on a bluff overlooking the sea.
Charlotte's bedroom—the same time.
Charlotte's paintings cover the walls and below her window, the sea crashes against the jagged rocks. Charlotte is stretched across the bed in an oversized t-shirt talking on the phone.
CHARLOTTE – So how does it feel to be a Steinmann semi-finalist?

Downstairs den in Charlotte's parents' house.
Miles is standing in front of a wet bar taking out champagne glasses as he talks on the phone.
MILES – It feels good so far.

Charlotte's bedroom—same time.
Charlotte giggles as she doodles on a piece of paper.
CHARLOTTE – I'm really excited for you!

Downstairs den—same time
Miles takes out a bottle of champagne from the wet bar fridge.
MILES – Thanks. Maybe we could celebrate together.

Charlotte's bedroom—same time.

Charlotte closes her eyes and snuggles under the covers.

CHARLOTTE – When?

MILES (O.S.) – I don't know. I'll call you.

CHARLOTTE – Okay.

Charlotte hangs up the phone and burrows deep under the covers. She opens her eyes as the doorknob turns slowly. She smiles as Miles stands in the doorway with the bottle of champagne and two glasses in his hand.

CHARLOTTE – That was fast.

Miles puts the champagne down, walks over to the bed, and kisses her slowly on the lips.

MILES – Yep.

Then he kicks off his shoes and jacket and dives into the bed on top of Charlotte. Charlotte laughs and pretends to hide under the covers.

MILES – You can run, but you can't hide!

He dives under the spread and starts to cover her face with playful kisses. Still giggling she holds him tightly, pressing her lips against his.

Outside Peabody Terrace—later that night.

The professor is lifted onto a stretcher. A paramedic throws blankets around Summer and the three other women. Suddenly we hear the sound of running feet and we see J.P. panting and out of breath as he rushes over to Summer. He gathers her in his arms and holds her tightly.

J.P. –Thank God you're okay.

Still numb and shaken, Summer can barely speak as tears fall down her face.

SUMMER – How did you know what happened?

Looking guilty and pained, J.P. gently guides her away from the crowd to a quiet corner.

J.P. – I don't know how to say this.

SUMMER – What're you talking about?

J.P. – I was trying to help you get over your fear of falling.

SUMMER –What!?

J.P. – The elevator was only supposed to fall three floors, I don't know what happened.

Summer looks at him as if she can't believe what she's hearing. Suddenly consumed with rage, she starts beating her fists against him.

SUMMER – How could you!?

He tries to take her in his arms but she pushes him away roughly and runs from him. J.P. stands by helplessly and then sinks to the ground, burying his head in his hands.

Nathan's bedroom—one week later.

As Nathan sits at his desk studying, J.P. sticks his head in the door.

J.P. – Did you take Physics 230 last year?

NATHAN – What about it?

J.P. – I was wondering if you still had a copy of the midterm exam.

NATHAN – No. But I remember the questions.

J.P. – Well, if you could give em to me later I'd appreciate it. I won't bother you now.

J.P. starts to leave.

NATHAN – What's this stuff about you guys wanting to call off the fear thing?

J.P. – We just thought that after what happened on the elevator, but you should talk to Miles and Summer.

NATHAN – So you're still into it?

J.P. turns away hesitantly from Nathan's stare, but says nothing.

Outside Summer's dormitory—the next day.

J.P. jumps out of his car and takes out a huge bouquet of flowers in one hand and a large shopping bag in the other. He then walks up a narrow flight of stairs to her dorm room.

He knocks on the door and Summer answers. When she opens it, her hair is in a bun, a pencil in her mouth and a textbook in her hand. She looks at him coldly.

SUMMER – What?

J.P. – You mind if I come in?

Summer stands to the side and lets him in. As J.P. walks in, he hands Summer the flowers. He walks into her kitchen and puts the bag on the table.

J.P. – I'm sorry.

Summer leans on the refrigerator.

J.P. – I didn't mean any harm. I was just trying to help you get over your fear, but I messed up. When the professor got on, it threw the formula off.

Summer softens a little.

J.P. – That's the honest to God truth.

J.P. turns to leave.

SUMMER – Wait, you forgot your bag.

J.P. – It's for you.

J.P. reaches into the bag, takes out a pound of Godiva chocolate, a gallon of Haagen Dazs ice cream, a bottle of Kahlua, and a can of New Orleans Cafe Du Monde coffee. Summer smiles.

SUMMER – Thank you.

She walks over to J.P. and kisses him on the lips.

SUMMER – Why don't you stay?

J.P. smiles.

J.P. – Sure.

Inside Charlotte's car driving up to Faneuil Hall—three weeks later.

Brightly colored Christmas decorations stand out against the snow-covered buildings. Miles and Charlotte are zooming along in her Fiat. The music is jamming.

MILES – One month before Christmas.
CHARLOTTE – Thank God.
Miles kisses Charlotte.
CHARLOTTE – Are you ready to celebrate your birthday?
Miles grins.
MILES – What did you have in mind?
CHARLOTTE – You'll see!

Inside a biology lab on campus—same time.
The room is empty except for Nathan, who is working at a back table. In front of him is a large cage with two laboratory rats playfully scratching each other and pushing against the sides of the cage. There are two syringes and a bottle of white solution in front of Nathan.

Nathan carefully opens the cage and pulls out one of the rats by the back of its neck. While clutching the squirming rat in one hand, he picks up a syringe with the other hand, pokes the needle in the bottle of solution and fills the syringe. He then injects the rat behind its ear. Almost immediately, the rat stops struggling and appears immobilized. Nathan then takes the second syringe and slides the sharp needle into the rat's abdomen. It's eyes blink, but there is no other reaction.

Nathan looks up as the lab door opens. A janitor pulling a bucket of soapy water and a mop comes in the room.

The janitor walks over to the table where Nathan is working and peers curiously into the cage. The rat Nathan injected is lying motionless on its side.

JANITOR – He don't look too good.

Nathan glances at the rat and seeing that it's dead, picks it up by the tail and tosses it in the trash.

NATHAN – I guess practice makes perfect.

Diamond Bluff—later that evening.

Charlotte parks her car next to a large tree. She walks over to the edge of the bluff followed by Miles. Below them, the sea rolls and churns against the rocks.

MILES – This is the best birthday I've ever had.

Charlotte stands behind Miles encircling her arms around his waist and kissing him on the back of the neck.

CHARLOTTE – The other night I dreamed that we decided to spend the rest of our lives together. I remember getting up in the morning with a huge smile on my face.

Miles blushes.

CHARLOTTE – I hope I'm not making you nervous.

MILES – No. I'd like that very much.

He kisses her, then unclasps the chain around his neck and hands Charlotte the ring that's on the chain.

MILES – Here...I want you to have this.

Charlotte takes it in surprise.

MILES – It was my mother's wedding band. My father gave it to me after she died.

CHARLOTTE – Oh Miles, you can't give me your mother's ring!

MILES – I want to.

Tears well up in Charlotte's eyes and she hugs him.

CHARLOTTE – I love you.

MILES I love you, too.

He holds her tightly and then reluctantly breaks away.

MILES – I guess we should head back. I told J.P. we'd meet him at Henry's.

They walk arm in arm back to her car.

Inside Henry's parents' house—later that night.

A jamming party. The prep elite goes hip hop. No ordinary set. Plush furniture, polished white wood floors, and brilliant splashes of abstract art. People everywhere. Lounging, swinging, and bopping to the ceaseless beat. Floor to ceiling windows reveal the teal blue waters of an indoor pool. Silence. Then a crash as the waters part and a nude woman dives in.

Charlotte grabs Miles's hand as they follow Summer around the expensively furnished room.

MILES – Whoa, this house is serious!

SUMMER – Can you believe Henry's parents let him have a party while they're out of town?

A friend comes up behind Miles, draping his arm around Miles's shoulder.

FRIEND – What's up, boy? Ready to turn this mother out!

MILES – Think I ain't?

Miles gives him high five.

MILES – Give me a minute, I'll put our coats up.

The music is blasting as Miles weaves through the massive sea of bodies moving to the beat.

He picks his way around people lounging on the stairs and opens the bedroom door at the top of the stairs. Coats are piled high on the bed and the floor. As he tosses the coats on the bed, he notices Nathan and J.P. standing against a wall partially obscured by a carved armoire.

MILES – Hey, what's up?

J.P. – peers out from around the armoire.

J.P. – Yo.

Miles wanders in and sees J.P. take a quick hit from a vial and then hand it back to Nathan.

MILES – Oh, sorry.

J.P. – It's cool. Come on in.

MILES – I'll just be a second.

Miles puts his things on the bed and starts to leave but Nathan walks toward him, showing Miles the vial.

NATHAN (to Miles) – Are you into it?

MILES – What do you mean?

NATHAN – Do you get high?

MILES – Not really.

Nathan throws Miles the vial.

NATHAN – Well try it, a mind excursion can be such a thrill.

Miles looks at the vial curiously.

MILES – So this is how you guys spend your allowance?

J.P. – Among other things.

NATHAN – Hold on.

Nathan closes the door and J.P. leans against it so no one can walk in. Nathan scoops out a small amount from the vial on a spoon and holds it up to Miles's nose. Miles takes a tentative hit in both nostrils.

MILES – Oooh, that stings!

Henry's living room—a few minutes later.

Charlotte, Summer, and two other women are lounging on the couch. They're falling all over each other laughing at something that Summer has just said. Nathan stumbles through the room brandishing a bottle of tequila. He heads over to Charlotte and the other women, waving the bottle dramatically.

NATHAN – Shots anyone?

Charlotte giggles and holds up her glass.

CHARLOTTE – I'll take some.

SUMMER – Me, too.

Nathan sloshes tequila in their glasses and turns to the other women.

NATHAN – Okay, your turn, all of you.

Nathan pours tequila in all of their glasses.

NATHAN – Now okay. Everybody, one, two, three . . .

Laughing and giggling as they all try and down the tequila in one gulp.

Upstairs hallway—minutes later.

J.P.'s hands roam over a woman's bare back. She shudders with pleasure and whispers something to him.

He takes her hand and they duck into a bedroom, shutting the door firmly behind them.

Side of indoor pool—same time.

Miles meanders around the side of the pool. Heads bobbing up and down in the water, churning to the heavy bass beat of the music.

Miles dives in. Resurfacing, he lazily floats on his back to the other end of the pool. Around him, people scream with laughter as two guys throw in a fully dressed woman.

Top of stairs—same time.

J.P. stands at the top of the stairs with his arm lightly around a woman. They start down the stairs, but his foot twists on a paper cup and they tumble to the bottom. She falls on top of him. Hands pull her up. She leans over J.P. seductively.

WOMAN – Get up lazy...

Still leaning over, she offers him her hand. J.P. smirks and grabs her hand.

WOMAN – C'mon, I wanna dance.

She runs her foot up his leg teasingly. J.P. stiffens and his smile freezes.

J.P. – Do that again.

She runs her foot along his leg again.

J.P. – I can't feel anything in my legs!

Panicking, she kneels down and starts rubbing his legs hard.

WOMAN – Are you sure?

J.P. *(hysterically)* – Just get a doctor! There's no feeling, nothing!

Nathan has rushed over and leans down whispering.

NATHAN – It's okay. It'll wear off. *(To the woman)* Just get him some water.

Still scared, the woman hesitates, but Nathan yells at her impatiently.

NATHAN – Now!

The music booms, drowning out her response as she runs off. Shaking with anger, J.P. glares at Nathan.

J.P. – You're a jerk! We said it was over!

Poolside—same time.

Through the shimmering water, Miles lies motionless at the bottom of the pool. Two men frantically dive in. Grabbing him. Dragging his lifeless body to the surface. The crowd parts as three people hoist Miles's limp body to the side. A man pries Miles's mouth open and begins to give him mouth-to-mouth resuscitation.

Charlotte pushes her way frantically through the crowd and leans down next to him shaking and crying bitterly. The man performing the mouth-to-mouth resuscitation is trying even harder now.

CHARLOTTE – Oh Miles...

Miles chokes. Spitting up water. And his eyes open slowly.

Outside Henry's house—later.

People leave the party quickly. The mood is tense and the only talking is muffled and hurried. We see a friend helping Miles, who's walking shakily. J.P. comes over to Charlotte and motions her aside to talk.

We don't hear their conversation, but we see Charlotte lean heavily against a car and then shake her head in disbelief. She slowly walks off. Her eyes search the crowd. She sees Nathan, who hurries over to her, but before he can say anything, she slaps him hard and runs toward Miles.

Upstairs bedroom—Henry's house—later.

Nathan leans over a desk and snorts a line of cocaine. A couple of blotters (tabs of acid) sit next to the tray.

As he finishes, Summer rushes in angrily. He turns and tries to obscure her view of the cocaine.

NATHAN – I thought you were leaving.

SUMMER – I was. But we need to talk.

NATHAN – Look, I don't have anything to say, okay?

SUMMER – Nathan, what if Miles or J.P. had died?

NATHAN – But they didn't.

Summer stands in front of Nathan, seething.

SUMMER – Are you crazy?

NATHAN – They were both drunk; don't blame that on me.

Summer faces him off but he turns away. Then she notices the mirror behind his back.

SUMMER – What are you doing?

NATHAN – None of your business.

She walks over to the mirror and sees the lines of cocaine.

SUMMER – And I thought you'd quit!

NATHAN – I lied.

SUMMER – Nathan, you're killing yourself.

NATHAN – I told you to get outta here!

Summer blows the cocaine into the wind. Nathan slaps Summer hard.

NATHAN – Have you lost your mind!?

Her face reddens and she slaps him back. Nathan grabs her and pushes her against the wall.

NATHAN – Yeah, right.

He throws her on the bed. She picks herself up and stalks out of the room.

SUMMER – I hope you rot in hell!

Harvard University Dean of Students office—one week later. A grandfather clock ticks in the background. The Dean of Students impatiently drums his fingers across the top of his desk. J.P. looks down at the ground as if wishing this were just a bad dream.

DEAN – Unfortunately, your telephone number has shown up on a short list of possibilities that could've caused the elevator override.

J.P. – looks at him stunned.

J.P. – There must be some mistake.

DEAN – I sincerely hope so.

J.P. tries to avoid the Dean's piercing stare.

DEAN – If for some reason, however, you did have anything to do with this matter, I urge you to cooperate so that it doesn't cause irreparable harm to your future.

J.P. looks down but says nothing.

Student Union lockers—later that same day.

J.P. and Miles stand by their lockers silently, stuffing books in their knapsacks. As Miles crams the last of his things in his backpack, he turns to J.P. slowly.

MILES – Are you going to be all right?

J.P. – I don't know. I'm scared about this elevator thing.

MILES – What are you gonna do?

J.P. – There's nothin' I can do.

J.P. sinks down to the ground, worried.

MILES – How's your back?

J.P. – You tell me.

J.P. stands up, pulls up his shirt, and we see huge black and blue marks from where he fell down the stairs at the party.

MILES – What'd the doctor say?

J.P. – I didn't go.

MILES – Are you crazy? That looks pretty bad.

J.P. – What would I say? "I fell down the stairs 'cause I was high"?

MILES – You don't have to tell 'em everything.

J.P. – Well, I'm just gonna wait and see if it gets better.

They walk a short distance in silence.

MILES – Nathan's an asshole.

J.P. – No kidding.

Miles sits down on a hall bench.

MILES – Maybe someone should show him the light.

J.P. leans intently over Miles.

J.P. – So you think it's time he confronts his fear?

MILES – All I know is I'm not taking this thing lying down.

J.P. – Well, if you're into it, I've got an idea.

J.P.'s room—a few days later.

J.P. carefully loads three chambers of a small gun with bullets from a box marked BLANKS. We hear Nathan's door slam. J.P. quickly closes the gun and slides it into the table drawer in front of him.

He then takes the box of BLANKS, puts them in a small bag next to him, and shoves it under his bed.

Charlotte's room—same day.

Charlotte lets herself into her dorm. She wanders into her bedroom and notices her answering machine light blinking. She presses it.

ANSWERING MACHINE (computerized voice) – You have one message.

The sound of someone hanging up the phone on the answering machine. As Charlotte pushes rewind, her phone rings. She picks it up.

CHARLOTTE – Hello?

VOICE – Charlotte Gainsworth?

CHARLOTTE – Yes.

VOICE – Hi, this is Kathleen from Harvard Health services.

Charlotte tenses. The nurse continues quickly.

VOICE – Your test results are in and Dr. Rosa would like to schedule an appointment to speak with you in person. How's Thursday at ten?

Charlotte is quiet.

VOICE – Is that okay?

CHARLOTTE – Yeah, it's fine.

Charlotte lays the receiver in its cradle. As she sinks onto the bed, a tear rolls down her cheek.

Near J.P.'s car—same time.

Miles and J.P. emerge from the shadows and climb into J.P.'s car. Miles is dressed completely in black.

Inside Charlotte's dorm room—same time.

Charlotte lies motionless on her bed. After a few minutes, she reaches for the phone and dials. Busy. She dials again. Still busy. Charlotte twirls the ring on the chain around her neck. Pulling herself off the bed, she grabs her coat and heads for the door.

J.P.'s car outside Nathan and J.P.'s apartment—same time.

J.P. shuts the motor off. Miles pulls on a black ski mask.

MILES – Gimme a few minutes to get in.

J.P. – Don't worry, I got your back.

Miles gives J.P. a high five and opens the car door.

Outside Miles's dorm—moments later.

Charlotte leans against the open door talking to Miles's roommate.

ROOMMATE – You missed him by maybe 15-20 minutes. I think he said that he was going to Nathan's.

CHARLOTTE – Did he say when he'd be back?

The roommate shakes his head.

ROOMMATE – No, sorry.

Phone booth across the street from J.P. and Nathan's apartment—same time.
J.P. slides the door shut and dials.
J.P. – Nathan, it's J.P. Listen up. I was on my way in and I saw someone checking out the apartment—it looks like they're trying to break in.

Nathan's room—same time.
Nathan turns off the light and slowly parts the curtains. From his point of view, we see a male figure edging around the building.
NATHAN – I see him.

Phone booth—same time.
J.P. – Look, the gun my ole man gave me is in my table drawer.
NATHAN – Okay.

J.P.'s bedroom—minutes later.
The room is dark except for the streetlight outside the window. Nathan carefully opens J.P.'s drawer and takes out the gun. He opens it and notices three empty chambers. He quickly sifts through the drawer looking for more bullets. Nothing.
He opens the drawer above, grabbing impatiently at papers. His fingers curve around a small box marked BULLETS. He pulls out the unopened box of bullets. Tearing it open, he shoves three more bullets into the gun, spins the chamber, and closes the gun.

J.P. and Nathan's kitchen—same time.
A window opens. A black gloved hand reaches in and slowly pushes the door open. Miles creeps into the kitchen. He strains for sounds. Silence.

J.P.'s bedroom—same time.
Nathan flattens himself against the wall. Through the crack in the door, he sees the partial reflection of a black-masked figure walking out of the kitchen. Nathan checks the gun again.

Living room.
The camera follows Miles as he walks slowly toward Nathan's room. It's dark. The covers piled high, like someone sleeping. But no movement. He walks carefully back into the living room.

J.P.'s room.
Nathan watches the figure through the crack in the door.
Living room.
Miles edges toward J.P.'s room.

J.P.'s room.
Miles creeps tentatively into the room. His eyes sweep the room. Then a dull thud, and searing pain in Miles's temples as the gun butt is whacked across his head.
From Miles's point of view, the room starts to cloud and tumble. He sees Nathan standing over him holding the gun. Miles lunges at Nathan's ankles and tackles him to the ground, slamming Nathan's head into the desk leg.
Nathan squeezes the trigger. The lamp shatters. Miles pins Nathan down grabbing for the gun. But Nathan pulls the trigger again. The sound of the gun firing pierces the air.
Miles doubles over in pain and rolls off Nathan. Nathan shoots the gun again at close range. The sound of footsteps running into the room. J.P., breathing hard and shaking bursts into the room.
J.P. – Whaddyou do. Are you okay?
Nathan still trembling, nods. J.P. sees Miles's motionless body and freezes. He kneels slowly by the body and tears off the ski mask. Nausea creeps over Nathan as he sees Miles's face.

NATHAN – Damn! It's Miles.

J.P. quickly grabs the gun from Nathan's hand and opens the chamber. He blinks and turns pale. Three chambers fired, three not fired.

J.P. – How many times did you shoot him?

Nathan drops to the ground and places his head against Miles's chest, willing him to breathe. Nothing.

NATHAN – I don't think he's breathing.

Nathan is numbly holding his knees against his chest, shaking in disbelief.

J.P. yells in aggravation.

J.P. – You killed him!

NATHAN – It's not my fault. He was trying to kill me!

J.P. – Wake up, Nathan. Who's gonna believe you?

NATHAN – You've gotta help me.

J.P. paces back and forth angrily hitting his fist against the wall.

J.P. – Ok, lemme think. I don't know what to do. We should just call the police.

NATHAN – No, wait. Wait, I have an idea. Let's dump the body.

J.P. – Are you out of your mind? Dump a body?

NATHAN – Listen. At the mouth of the Charles. Right under the bridge. Nobody will know.

J.P. – No way! I can't do that!

NATHAN – If you don't, the Dean's gonna find out who made that elevator fall.

J.P. sits on the floor, with a trapped look on his face.

J.P. – All right. Just get a sheet and help me put him in the car.

J.P. and Nathan carry Miles's limp body into J.P's car and place him in the trunk. J.P. slams the door and roars off.

Charlotte's car—same time.

Charlotte clutches the steering wheel. She veers sharply, barely missing an oncoming car. Shaking, she continues on.

Nathan's apartment—moments later.

The apartment is dark. Nathan is sitting numbly on the floor. Tears run down his cheeks. A car's headlights glide across the room.

Charlotte bangs on the door. The door opens. Her eyes strain against the misty black. She walks through the living room, peering in Nathan's and then J.P.'s room. Charlotte jumps in surprise. Nathan is sitting in the dark on the floor.

CHARLOTTE – Nathan? Why didn't you answer the door?

She walks over to the table and turns on a lamp. Her eyes travel to Nathan's terrified face. The rug in front of him has a large irregular damp reddish spot. The room is a mess. Shattered glass, chairs, books knocked over. And next to him a gun.

CHARLOTTE – What happened to your head? You're bleeding!

Nathan just stares at Charlotte numbly.

NATHAN – It wasn't my fault. I didn't mean to do it.

CHARLOTTE – What are you talking about?

NATHAN – He tried to kill me.

CHARLOTTE – Who are you talking about?

Nathan's voice breaks.

NATHAN – I. . . I didn't know it was him.

Charlotte's body goes numb. She digs her fingers into Nathan's shoulders, turning him toward her and forcing his eyes into hers.

CHARLOTTE – Where's Miles? Where's Miles? Nathan.

NATHAN – I didn't mean to kill him. You gotta believe me!

Charlotte beats her fists against Nathan. He sits motionless.

CHARLOTTE – Oh my God! Where is he? Where is he?

NATHAN – J.P. took him off Storrow Drive under the bridge.

CHARLOTTE – I hate you!

Charlotte runs out of the apartment.

J.P.'s car—immediately following.

J.P. is parked by the side of the road, lookingpale and shaken. Miles is standing by the car. Ripping at the buttons on his shirt, he opens it and pulls out a punctured plastic vest where sacs of fake blood have burst.

J.P. – Dang, you scared me. For a minute I thought you were really dead.

MILES – I thought you put blanks in the gun!

J.P. – I did! Nathan must've put in real ones.

MILES – That was close.

Miles climbs in the front seat.

MILES – Lets get outta here. I need to call Charlotte.

Under a bridge on the Charles River.

Charlotte stumbles along the bank of the river, searching for signs of J.P and Miles. But there's only darkness and quiet. She struggles up to the side of the road to a phone booth. She dials. An answering machine picks up.

MACHINE (O.S.) – Hi, this is Miles. At the beep it's your turn to speak.

Charlotte hangs up. Tearfully she thumbs through the phone book and dials again.

OPERATOR – Mass. General. May I help you?

CHARLOTTE – I'm looking for a Miles Broussard. He may have checked in through the emergency room.

College bar—night.

Loud. A raucous crowd. J.P. is at the bar with two mugs of beer in front of him. Miles walks up.

J.P. – Yo.

J.P. slides a beer to Miles, who is obviously preoccupied.

MILES – She's still not home.

J.P. – You leave a message?

MILES – Yeah. I left a message telling her what happened and that I was okay.

J.P. – Then cool ya jets. I'm sure she's just fine.

J.P. takes a long satisfying gulp of beer and holds his glass up for a toast.

J.P. – To bustin' out Nathan big time!

They clink their glasses together. Miles relaxes a little and takes a sip of beer.

Phone booth—later.

Charlotte's index finger travels to the bottom of a page of hospital listings. She lays down the phone book, fishes through her purse, and then dumps the contents on the phone ledge.

A quarter tumbles out. She picks it up and dials. Charlotte's eyes are red and puffy from crying.

OPERATOR (O.S.) – Boston Medical Center.

CHARLOTTE – I'm looking for a . . . Miles Broussard.

OPERATOR (O.S.) – Hold on. . . . No, I don't see anybody by that name admitted tonight. Have you tried Mercy or Charity?

CHARLOTTE – I've tried them all.

Charlotte hangs up the phone and walks dazedly back to her car.

College bar—later.

The place has thinned out. Miles turns to J.P., looking worried.

MILES – Can I borrow your car?

J.P. – Sure.

Charlotte's car—immediately following.

Charlotte leans her head against the steering wheel and cries bitterly.

Charlotte's parents' summer home—later.

Charlotte pulls up in front of her parents' summer home. She huddles under her coat in the pelting snow and stumbles to the front door.

J.P.'s car outside the bar—same time.
Miles turns on the windshield wipers, trying to scrape off the cascades of snow. He tries to pull away but the wheels won't move in the snow. Miles bangs his hand against the steering wheel. He turns on the ignition and floors the accelerator, but there is only the screeching of the wheels stuck in the snow.

Charlotte's home—same time.
Numbly, Charlotte undresses. She throws a thin robe around her shoulders and walks into the kitchen. She pours herself a glass of wine and sits motionless at the window staring at the steadily falling snow.

J.P.'s car—same time.
Miles is outside the car scraping snow away from the wheels. But the snow is now falling so thickly that each time he scrapes some snow away, gusts of wind blow more snow under the wheels.

Charlotte's home—hours later.
The snow has stopped. Miles screeches up in J.P.'s car. Charlotte's car is covered with snow. He walks to the front door and knocks but Charlotte doesn't respond. He knocks again and the door creaks open.
MILES – Charlotte, it's me . . .
Miles follows the sound of a radio up the stairs to the second floor.
MILES – Charlotte . . .

He walks into Charlotte's room. The covers are thrown back but the room is empty. He turns off the radio and walks down the hallway into the master bedroom following the sound of the steady drip of water. Slowly he opens the door.

The sound of running water is louder. Breathing hard, he flings open the bathroom door. He sees water spilling over the side of the bathtub, pooling up in dark circles on the floor.

Charlotte's robe is lying in a heap, soaked through with water. He stoops, picking it up carefully, and then letting it slip through his fingers to the floor. Now he runs, down the hallway, frantically throwing open doors...

MILES – Charlotte!

But each room is empty and silent. He runs down the stairs into the living room. Stumbles on a shattered wine glass. His eyes blur as he runs into the kitchen. And stops. A tangled rope lies on the table. Then he sees the pantry door, shut tightly with a piece of fabric jammed in the door. Shaking, he opens the door. An apron swings in his face. Grinding his teeth, he pulls open the basement door.

Charlotte's limp body hangs from the rafter.

Questions and Model Answers

Question

You have fifty minutes to answer the following question based on the fact pattern above and on the law you reviewed in Section Ten.

Explain which crimes, if any, J.P. and his accomplice committed when they tampered with the elevator at Peabody Terrace. For the purposes of this question, you should assume that Nathan was J.P.'s accomplice. Your analysis of the law and how it applies to the facts is of primary importance, not merely picking the correct crimes that J.P. and/or Nathan may have committed. Remember, for purposes of this exercise, focus only on the crimes and not with each individual's defense.

Your Answer

_____

_____

_____

_____

_____

_____

_____

_____

_____

_____

_____

_____

_____

_____

_____

_____

_____

_____

_____

_____

_____

_____

_____

Model Answer

Model answers are for illustrative purposes only. They outline the relevant elements of the crimes found in the fact pattern and briefly raise some issues to discuss in an answer. Response to a real law school exam would, of course, include detailed analysis of various defenses to each crime and, thus, would be substantially longer.

J.P. and Nathan committed the following crimes: conspiracy, criminal trespass, and battery. In addition, if the professor fails to recover and dies, both J.P. and his accomplice would be guilty of murder under the felony murder doctrine or perhaps, involuntary manslaughter, depending upon the degree of intent established.

Conspiracy: To have a conspiracy, there must be an intentional agreement to commit an illegal objective by two or more persons. Facts indicate that both J.P. and Nathan were working together to alter the operation of the elevator. The two communicate by phone and, in fact, J.P. only acts once Nathan has given him the signal— Summer "just got on the elevator."

At no time does it appear that either J.P. or Nathan have been coerced into cooperating. Thus, their agreement appears to have been intentional. The underlying crime is criminal trespass.

The elements of trespass are (1) the intentional (2) violation of (3) another's (4) property.

In this case, the property was the elevator operational code that pertained to Peabody Terrace. J.P. and Nathan agreed to violate this property and gain access to the codes. We can argue that the property (the codes) was private because access was only allowed through a special combination. Thus, we have established that both J.P. and Nathan are guilty of a conspiracy to commit a criminal trespass.

Battery: A battery is the (1) intentional (2) unlawful (3) offensive touching of another or of an object that is an extension or an integral part of the person.

In the fact pattern, J.P. and Nathan conspire to break into the elevator codes to make it fall during its run. Their act of altering the code—causing the elevator to fall—could be considered as an offensive, unlawful touching of an object that was an extension or an integral part of the occupants' bodies.

Clearly, there was injury. Summer had to be resuscitated, the professor had to be carried out on a stretcher, and each elevator occupant had to be helped off by the medics.

There also was causation. If not for the defendants' (J.P. and Nathan) act, injury would not have occurred. Moreover, injury was the reasonably foreseeable result of the defendants' actions. Thus, the elements establishing battery are present in this fact pattern.

Felony Murder: Both J.P. and Nathan may be guilty of murder under the felony murder doctrine if the professor dies from her injuries. To have a murder, there must be an intentional killing of another without adequate, legal justification. For someone to be guilty under the felony murder doctrine, the murder must have been committed during the commission of a felony and was a reasonably foreseeable result of the felony. There are many ways to establish intent. Intent can be presumed if the defendant killed the person without the existence of an adequate provocation or if the defendant had lain in wait to kill the victim.

Intent can also be established if the defendant was guilty of extremely reckless and wanton behavior with a total disregard for the well-being and safety of others. In this example, it could be argued that J.P. and Nathan's conduct was both extremely reckless and wanton with a total disregard for the well-being and safety of the elevator occupants. Because of their conduct, it was foreseeable that an accident might occur and that someone might die as a result. In this case, that someone may be the professor carried away on a stretcher. If the professor dies, J.P. and Nathan are guilty of murder under the felony murder doctrine.

J.P. and Nathan could, in the alternative, be found guilty of involuntary manslaughter if their behavior was found to be criminally negligent rather than extremely reckless with a disregard for the victim. Involuntary manslaughter is a lesser criminal offense than murder.

Question

Take one hour to answer this two-part question.

Part 1: Nathan committed several crimes when he offered the drugs to Miles and J.P. Assume that Miles drowned, and Nathan is standing trial for his death. As the prosecution, what would be your arguments for seeking a murder conviction?

Part 2 : Next, assume that you are Nathan's defense attorney and must give arguments to reduce the murder charge to involuntary manslaughter. What would be your arguments?

Your Answer

_____

_____

_____

_____

_____

_____

_____

_____

_____

_____

_____

_____

_____

_____

_____

_____

_____

_____

_____

_____

_____

_____

_____

_____

_____

_____

_____

_____

_____

_____

_____

_____

_____

_____

_____

_____

_____

_____

_____

_____

_____

_____

_____

_____

_____

_____

_____

_____

_____

_____

_____

Model Answer

Part 1: Murder is the (1) deliberate, intentional (2) act of one (3) killing someone without legal justification.

The death must be the result of the deliberate act and there must be concurrence between the act and the intent during commission of the crime.

Intent To convict Nathan for the murder of Miles Broussard, we must show that he had the requisite intent to kill the victim. During the party, Nathan deliberately offered Miles the vial containing the deadly substance. Nathan knew of the danger, yet at no time did he warn Miles. In fact, he encouraged Miles to try the drug when he: (1) tossed the vial to Miles and (2) stated "[w]ell, try it." These are not cautionary words, but instead reflect the state of mind of someone deliberately intending to kill another.

We can also establish the requisite intent because the facts also show that Nathan was in a biology lab, presumably concocting the deadly substance. Thus, he deliberately and in a premeditated fashion prepared the deadly drug, brought it to the party where he knew Miles would be, and offered and, indeed, encouraged Miles to inhale a substance that he knew to be lethal. These facts establish that Nathan had the requisite intent to commit murder.

Act and causation Intent alone cannot convict a person of murder; one must establish an act that caused the death, while the person maintained the necessary intent. Nathan did act while having the requisite mens rea.

The act was the offering of the vial containing the poisonous substance to Miles. This act led directly to Miles's death. There was no intervening event to break the chain of causation and Miles's death was the reasonably foreseeable result of Nathan's giving Miles the poisonous vial and urging him to try it. Nathan's actions also occurred during the time of his intent to kill Miles, satisfying the concurrence requirement.

The facts of this case establish the existence of necessary elements to convict Nathan of the crime of murder.

Part 2: As Nathan's defense attorney, you could interpret the facts in such a way to argue that Nathan did not commit murder.

Nathan did not have the requisite premeditated, deliberate intent to kill Miles, and thus, to be convicted of murder. He could, perhaps, be convicted of involuntary manslaughter.

The requisite intent for murder is not present. Nathan did not "lie in wait" for Miles nor was his intent premeditated. He did not expect Miles to come into the room, nor did he create a trap to entice Miles to enter the room. Because Nathan was surprised by Miles's appearance, he could not have formed the necessary premeditated intent required for murder. Due to his reckless behavior, however, a death resulted. Since the requisite intent is not present to establish murder, Nathan's charge should be reduced to involuntary manslaughter.

To establish involuntary manslaughter, there must have been (1) an act (2) of criminal negligence or extremely reckless behavior to substitute for intent (3) causation.

The act was Nathan offering the poisonous vial to Miles. The offering of a vial was, at a minimum, extremely reckless. Such behavior might be considered evidence of a wanton disregard for human life, in which case, the requisite intent for murder would be presumed. Although possibly not intended, Nathan's act directly caused Miles's death. The elements exist to find Nathan guilty of involuntary manslaughter. Without the mens rea necessary for murder, Nathan could not be found guilty of that crime.

Question

You have twenty minutes to answer both parts of this question.

Part 1: Nathan urges his friends to participate in an exercise to overcome their fears. If this exercise involved the commission of a crime, what crime would Nathan be guilty of?

Part 2: What would Summer, Nathan, Miles, and J.P. be guilty of if they agreed to participate in the criminal enterprise and took initial steps to execute the plan?

Your Answer

_____

_____

_____

_____

_____

_____

_____

_____

_____

_____

Model Answer

Part 1: Assuming that the fear exercise involved a criminal activity, Nathan would be guilty of solicitation. Solicitation is the (1) intentional urging of (2) another to (3) commit a crime.

Each element of the crime solicitation is present in the fact pattern. There is intentional urging—Nathan deliberately encourages his friends to confront their fears by participating in the game—and we have been told that the exercise will involve the commission of a crime.

Since the crime of solicitation does not require that the person or persons actually commit the crime, Nathan would be guilty of solicitation simply due to his encouragement of the others to engage in a criminal activity. Whether they finally agree to participate is irrelevant as to whether Nathan was guilty of solicitation.

Part 2: Each character, J.P., Miles, Nathan, and Summer, is guilty of the crime of conspiracy. The elements of conspiracy are (1) an intentional agreement (2) by two or more persons (3) to commit a crime or to accomplish a legal objective by illegal means.

We know that the fear exercise involves the commission of a criminal act. Assuming that each character is aware of this fact, they would be guilty of conspiracy because there was an intentional agreement by each (submitting the paper with their name and fear), and there were more than two participants. Remember that some jurisdictions require the commission of an overt action in furtherance of the conspiracy.

Question

You have thirty minutes to answer the following question.

How would you argue that Nathan committed a battery against J.P. during the party scene at Henry's house when Nathan offered J.P. the drugs?

Your Answer

_____

_____

_____

_____

_____

_____

_____

_____

_____

_____

_____

_____

_____

Model Answer

The key to proving battery in this question is to define Nathan's act of providing the drugs to J.P.—resulting in injury—as an offensive touching.

Battery is the (1) intentional or criminally negligent, unlawful (2) touching of (3) another (4) causing injury in an offensive manner.

The act is the touching. It must be intentional or criminally negligent. The injury does not necessarily have to be physical. Injury can be satisfied from the fact that the touching was offensive or offended the sensibilities of an ordinary person.

In the party scene, Nathan provides J.P. with a vial of a substance that ultimately causes temporary paralysis. Is it offensive touching to offer the vial?

A battery is committed if a person unlawfully and offensively touches any object that can be considered a part or extension of the injured person's body. Is it offensive touching when Nathan hands the vial to J.P.? Once J.P. takes the vial, it becomes an extension of his body. If Nathan had suddenly grabbed it out of J.P's hands, it would certainly be offensive touching for the purposes of establishing that a battery had been committed.

If we consider that a reasonable person would consider being offered a vial of a toxic substance offensive, particularly if they were unaware that it had been altered to cause an unexpected negative side effect, then Nathan's action could be considered offensive. Thus, we can argue that the offensive act was Nathan's offering of the vial to J.P. He did so intentionally or, at least, in a criminally negligent fashion, and the injury was J.P's temporary paralysis, as well as the injuries sustained during his fall. The injuries were the direct, foreseeable result of being offered the vial. Thus, Nathan would be guilty of battery.

Question

Answer the following question in ten minutes.

Apart from possession of an illegal substance, identify the crime(s) that Nathan and Summer commit in the scene immediately following Henry's party when Summer confronts Nathan about what he did to Miles and J.P. You should note that an individual has the right to self-defense when he or she reasonably believes that he or she is about to be, or is being, attacked. The force used must be that which is reasonably necessary to protect him or herself.

Your Answer

_____

_____

_____

_____

_____

_____

_____

_____

Model Answer

Nathan is guilty of committing battery against Summer when he initially slapped her. He also committed a second battery when he pushes her against the wall. The third battery occurs when he throws her to the bed. Summer did not commit a crime.

Battery is the (1) intentional or criminally negligent, unlawful (2) touching of (3) another (4) causing injury or in an offensive manner.

In that scene, Summer blows Nathan's cocaine away and Nathan "slaps Summer hard." The slap was not justified since it was not self-defense. Nathan could not have reasonably believed that he was in imminent danger of being attacked by Summer, due to Summer blowing away his cocaine. Nathan's blow was intentional, unjustified, and unlawful. The act was, of course, the slap itself, and the injury, was the direct result of or was caused by, the slap. As an alternative to establishing an injury, we could establish that the slap was offensive.

The second battery was committed when Nathan pushed Summer against the wall. Although Summer did slap him and afterward he threw her on the bed, his actions were not in self-defense, but were merely an unprovoked battery.

A person has the right to self-defense when he or she reasonably believes that they are going to be attacked. Summer slapped Nathan in self-defense since it was reasonable for her to protect herself. Nathan had just slapped her.

Thus, Summer is not guilty of a battery because she was protecting herself. She reasonably feared that she was going to be attacked (Nathan did attack her) and she employed reasonable force (a slap) to do so.

Nathan's subsequent throwing of Summer to the bed was an additional battery. This act was intentional and unjustified. Moreover, Nathan was not exercising his right to self-defense since Summer was only protecting herself against his attack.

Question

You have fifty minutes to answer each part of this question.

When Miles enters Nathan's apartment to make Nathan "confront his fear," does Miles commit a robbery? Does Miles commit a burglary, assault, battery, or extortion? Is J.P. guilty of any crimes?

Your Answer

_____

_____

_____

_____

_____

_____

_____

_____

_____

_____

_____

_____

_____

_____

_____

_____

_____

_____

_____

_____

_____

_____

_____

_____

_____

_____

Model Answer

Robbery

Miles does not commit a robbery. A robbery is defined as the (1) intentional, unlawful taking from another of (2) that person's personal property by (3) force or the threat of immediate force.

In the fact pattern, Miles did not attempt to take any item of personal property from Nathan. Since this element is not present, Miles could not have committed a robbery because every element must be present to be found guilty of that particular crime.

Although Miles does not commit a robbery, he does commit other crimes.

Other crimes

Miles does commit a burglary. A burglary is (1) the unlawful breaking and (2) entering of (3) a dwelling of (4) another with the (5) intent to commit a crime therein.

Under modern statutes, a breaking does not have to be a physical "breaking" or destruction of property to gain entrance. Simply entering the property is sufficient. Miles gained entry to Nathan's apartment, which constitutes the breaking (although he had J.P.'s acquiescence, he did not have Nathan's and Nathan was not aware of J.P.'s complicity).

The apartment is a dwelling and the facts show that it was not Miles's apartment. The crime that Miles intended to commit in the apartment was assault. Thus, Miles's intentional breaking into the dwelling place of another with the intent to commit a crime therein constitutes burglary for which he would be found guilty.

In addition to burglary, Miles also committed assault and battery.

To have an assault, we must find an intentional act that places the person in reasonable apprehension of imminent bodily harm.

Miles entered Nathan's apartment intending to commit an assault to provoke Nathan to shoot him. (We know that prior to leaving the apartment, J.P. loaded the gun with blank bullets, which they intended for Nathan to use against Miles.)

Miles also committed battery. A battery is the intentional, or criminally negligent, unlawful touching of another causing injury.

When Miles broke into the apartment, Nathan was reasonably placed in apprehension that harm would result. In response to this reasonable apprehension, he attempted to defend himself against the intruder. When Miles lunged at Nathan during the ensuing melee, he committed an intentional, unlawful, and offensive touching of Nathan—the battery.

Miles did not commit the crime of extortion. Extortion involves (1) obtaining someone's property (2) by a wrongful use or threat of force or coercion.

Although Miles may have used force to enter the apartment and later struggled with Nathan once he had gained entry, he did not do so to obtain property or to coerce Nathan to give him any property. As such, the necessary elements for the crime of extortion are not present and Miles is not guilty of committing that crime.

Miles and J.P.

Miles is also guilty of conspiracy. Conspiracy is an intentional agreement entered into by two or more people to commit a crime or a legal objective by illegal means. In some jurisdictions, an affirmative act in furtherance of the conspiracy is also required.

In the fact pattern, both Miles and J.P. intentionally agreed to assault Nathan as part of their fear game gone awry. Their agreement was to commit the illegal act of assaulting Nathan. Should the case be brought in a jurisdiction that requires an overt act to further the conspiracy, that overt act could be J.P.'s calling Nathan to warn him of an intruder (Miles), the breaking and entering of the apartment, or the assault itself. The call was perhaps the initial act setting in motion the illegal plan that they conspired to execute.

Question

You have ten minutes to answer this question.

When Miles entered J.P.'s and Nathan's apartment, did he commit the crime of false pretenses?

Your Answer

_____

_____

_____

_____

_____

_____

_____

_____

_____

_____

Model Answer

Miles does not commit the crime of false pretenses. False pretenses is defined as the (1) obtaining of title (2) to the personal property of another (3) by an intentional misrepresentation, with (4) the desire to defraud and deprive them of that property.

Miles did not obtain nor try to obtain title to another's personal property. Since this element is not present in the facts, Miles could not be found guilty of committing the crime of false pretenses.

Question

You have ten minutes to answer this question.

Suppose that Miles did not have the consent of either J.P. or Nathan the night he entered the apartment to make Nathan "face his fear." Of what crime is Miles guilty when he entered the apartment without consent and not necessarily to commit a crime therein?

Your Answer

_____

_____

_____

_____

_____

_____

_____

Model Answer

Since we assume that Miles did not intend to commit a crime inside the apartment, we cannot find Miles guilty of burglary. But if Miles did not have the consent of either J.P. or Nathan, he was guilty of trespass.

The elements of criminal trespass are the (1) intentional (2) invasion of (3) one's property.

When Miles entered the apartment without consent, he was intentionally invading, or committing a trespass.

Question

You have fifty minutes to answer this question.

Summer was severely shaken when the elevator fell, and J.P. and Miles were similarly injured during the pool party. All injuries were the result of the "fear exercise," which grew increasingly dangerous and life threatening. Throughout the exercise, each participant committed several crimes.

You are a prosecutor for the State of Massachusetts seeking to charge each character, except Miles, with felony murder for the death of Charlotte Gainsworth under the felony murder doctrine and with conspiracy. How would you present your case? Against whom would the charges be the weakest and why?

You should note that to exit a conspiracy, the person must clearly and unequivocally state their intention to no longer participate and they must take steps to prevent the furtherance of the conspiracy.

Your Answer

_____

_____

_____

_____

_____

_____

_____

_____

_____

_____

_____

_____

_____

_____

_____

_____

_____

_____

_____

_____

_____

_____

_____

_____

_____

_____

_____

_____

_____

_____

Model Answer

Under the felony murder doctrine, a defendant can be found guilty for any death that occurs during the commission of a felony. The felony must be the proximate cause of the death; the death must have been the reasonably foreseeable result of the felony.

To convict each of the characters other than Miles for felony murder under the felony murder doctrine, the murder must have been a foreseeable result of their felony. The issue, therefore, is to determine the underlying felony, whether each character was a co-conspirator in the commission of the felony and whether Charlotte's death was a foreseeable result of the felony.

Were Summer, J.P., and Nathan co-conspirators to commit the underlying felony that was the proximate cause of Charlotte's death? If the underlying felony is Miles's assault and battery with a dangerous weapon, Summer alone may not be guilty of felony murder because she was not a party to that conspiracy. If, however, you were a prosecutor attempting to convict each student of felony murder under the felony murder doctrine, you could argue that the underlying felony occurred long before the burglary and that Charlotte's death was, in fact, reasonably foreseeable given the increasingly violent nature of the game.

A conspiracy is the intentional agreement by two or more persons to commit an illegal objective or to commit a legal one by illegal means. When each student initially agreed to participate in the fear game, they were not entering into a conspiracy. Their agreement became a conspiracy as illegal means were used to achieve ostensibly legal objectives (to help one another overcome their fears). The first such illegal act was the criminal trespass into the elevator codes. The result of that was the injury to Summer and the other occupants.

After the accident occurred, each of the friends knew that it was the result of their fear game but none openly refused to participate and none took steps to prevent the conspiracy from continuing. In fact, Summer concealed evidence of the game/conspiracy from the school authorities when questioned. Thus, she not only took insufficient steps to exit the conspiracy, but by concealing evidence, she took affirmative steps to allow the conspiracy to continue.

After Summer's injury, J.P. is stricken by the temporary paralysis drug given to him by Nathan, and Miles nearly drowns due to his inhaling of the drug. This could be considered another step in furtherance of the conspiracy since it too was an attempt to achieve a legal objective (overcome fears) by illegal means (provide drugs and solicitation). Because of this incident, Miles, like Summer, could have easily died. Furthermore, the occurrence of these near-death incidents made the notion that someone may actually die due to the continuation of the conspiracy not only very plausible but also foreseeable.

Thus, even though all were aware that the injuries to Miles and J.P. were the direct result of their initial agreement, none made any effort to exit from the conspiracy or to prevent its furtherance. Instead, the students continued the conspiracy and simply concocted other schemes that made death more likely.

As a prosecutor attempting to convict each of the conspirators of felony murder for the death of Charlotte Gainsworth, you could, therefore, argue that her death was the reasonably foreseeable result of the conspiracy they each entered into at the outset and the series of felonies committed throughout. The chain of liability was never broken. As the conspiracy progressed and the underlying felonies grew more serious, death became an ever increasing, foreseeable possibility.

The charge of felony murder is weakest against Summer since she never participated in an exercise to rid someone of their fears. Thus, arguably, she never entered the conspiracy because her agreement at the outset was to participate in a game, not to commit illegal acts to obtain a legal objective (enter into a conspiracy). Moreover, in jurisdictions where an affirmative act is a required element of a conspiracy, Summer's failure to participate would protect her from criminal liability.

Question

You have ten minutes to answer this question.

When Nathan offered Miles the drugs, of what crime was he (Nathan) guilty?

Your Answer

_____

_____

_____

_____

_____

_____

_____

_____

_____

_____

_____

Model Answer

During the party scene, Nathan offered Miles the drugs, making him guilty of solicitation.

Solicitation is the (1) intentional urging of (2) another to (3) commit a crime.

It does not matter whether the person being urged actually committed the crime. All that is necessary to commit the crime is that you intentionally urged the person to commit it. In the scene, Nathan committed the crime of solicitation when he intentionally encouraged Miles to take illegal drugs. Even if Miles had declined to partake, Nathan would have been guilty.

Question

If Kovack, the Peabody Terrace superintendent, has a heart attack and dies while frantically attempting to enter a code to stop the elevator's free-fall, J.P. would be guilty of:

(a) battery
(b) involuntary manslaughter
(c) murder

Your Answer

_____

_____

_____

_____

Model Answer

(b) J.P. would be guilty of involuntary manslaughter. J.P's extremely reckless actions were the proximate cause of Kovack's death.

Question

Assume that in the elevator scene, the professor is taken away on a stretcher, never regains consciousness, and remains in critical condition in the hospital for several weeks. During a routine procedure, her doctor negligently administers an incorrect drug causing her death.

Choose the most correct answer.

(a) J.P. did not commit a crime.

(b) The doctor is not guilty of a crime because the professor was already in critical condition because of the elevator incident.

(c) The doctor and J.P. are jointly liable for the professors murder.

(d) J.P. is not guilty of murder.

Your Answer

_____

_____

_____

_____

_____

Model Answer

(d) Although J.P's actions were responsible for the professors original condition, the doctor's negligence was an intervening act that broke the chain of J.P's liability.

Question

Assume the professor is taken to the hospital and is immediately rushed to emergency surgery. Her husband agrees to the surgery. The attending doctor, who has been on call for the last thirty hours and is groggy, inadvertently cuts the nerves in her face, which results in a permanent, severe speech impediment, as well as severe deformity of the right side of her face. Because of the doctor's negligence, he is on trial and the jury should rule:

(a) guilty of battery
(b) innocent of mayhem
(c) guilty of mayhem
(d) guilty of both battery and mayhem

Your Answer

_____

_____

_____

_____

240 So You Want to Be a Lawyer

Model Answer

(b) The doctor is innocent of mayhem because the doctor did not intend to cause disfigurement of the professor. The question indicates that he "inadvertently" cut the nerves in her face. The doctor is not guilty of battery because there was consent to his "touching" of the professor. To constitute a battery, the "touching" must be unlawful. For the touching to be unlawful, there cannot be consent. When the professor's husband agreed to the surgery, this constituted consent to the "touching" and thus the jury could not find the doctor guilty of battery.

Question

When Nathan unexpectedly enters Charlotte's studio uninvited with dinner (where she and Miles were relaxing), has he committed a trespass? Yes or No.

Your Answer

_____

_____

_____

_____

_____

_____

_____

Model Answer

Yes. Nathan's entry was intentional and it was not his studio. He had not been invited in and, therefore, did not have consent or permission to enter the premises.

Question

When Charlotte kisses Miles after his recital for the Steinmann Fellowship, explain why she has not committed a battery.

Your Answer

_____

_____

_____

_____

_____

_____

_____

_____

Model Answer

Charlotte has not committed a battery because she had apparent consent to kiss Miles and thus her action could not be considered an unlawful or offensive touching.

Question

Assume that Charlotte had never met Miles, and under the facts presented in question 15, could Charlotte have been guilty of assault?

Your Answer

_____

_____

_____

_____

_____

_____

_____

_____

_____

Model Answer

Charlotte could only be charged with assault if by kissing Miles she put him in reasonable apprehension of imminent bodily harm. Since nothing in the facts suggests that he had reason to fear imminent bodily harm from her kiss, Charlotte would not be guilty of assault.

Question

The facts show that Nathan had plotted to temporarily paralyze J.P. He also nearly causes Miles to drown because of the same drug. Nathan, due to his extremely reckless behavior, is guilty of:

(a) conspiracy
(b) trespass
(c) mayhem
(d) none of the above

Your Answer

_____

_____

_____

_____

_____

_____

Model Answer

(d) There was no conspiracy. Nathan apparently acted on his own. There was no trespass since Nathan did not invade another's property and he did not commit mayhem—there was no disfigurement or dismemberment.

Question

A jury deliberating over whether Nathan is guilty of mayhem when he shot Miles after he broke into his apartment would find him guilty. True or False.

Your Answer

_____

_____

_____

_____

_____

_____

_____

_____

_____

_____

_____

_____

_____

_____

_____

_____

_____

_____

_____

_____

_____

_____

_____

_____

Model Answer

False. None of the elements of the crime of mayhem are present in the facts as given.

Question

Assume that Nathan, after slapping and throwing Summer on the bed, rips off her clothes, rubs his body against hers roughly, and beats her. He has committed:

(a) assault
(b) rape
(c) battery
(d) mayhem
(e) a and d only
(f) b and d only
(g) a and c only
(h) none of the above

Your Answer

_____

_____

_____

_____

_____

_____

Model Answer

(g) Nathan assaulted Summer and committed a battery. His actions were intentional. Summer was placed in reasonable apprehension that harm was imminent and Nathan unlawfully and offensively touched her. There was no rape, since for rape there must be penetration of the female sex organ by the male sex organ. There was no mayhem since there was no dismemberment by Nathan of any of Summer's bodily parts.

Question

You have five minutes to answer the following question.

After kissing Miles, Charlotte forces him, against his will, to have intercourse. Has Miles been raped?

Your Answer

_____

_____

_____

_____

_____

_____

_____

Model Answer

No. Miles has not been raped. Under common law, a woman cannot commit rape. The crime of rape under common law requires sexual intercourse with a woman by a man who is not her husband.

Question

After making Nathan confront his fear, J.P. takes Miles away by placing him in the trunk of his car. Although Miles agreed to participate in the overall scheme, he did not agree to being placed in the trunk. Has J.P. committed:

(a) mayhem
(b) assault
(c) false imprisonment
(d) kidnapping
(e) battery
(f) none of the above

Your Answer

_____

_____

_____

_____

_____

_____

Model Answer

(f) This question tests your ability to understand the elements of kidnapping. In kidnapping, you must confine the person *against his or her will,* by force or threat of force, or by deceit or fraud. Furthermore, the elements of concealment and transportation must be present. Although Miles is concealed and transported by J.P., the facts indicate that it is not against Miles's will since it was part of a scheme that Miles willingly participated in. Hence, J.P. did not kidnap Miles.

J.P.'S actions would not constitute false imprisonment for the same reasons he was not confined *against his will.*

Question

You have ten minutes to answer the following question.

Assume that instead of taking Miles away, J.P. takes Nathan out of the room and locks Miles in against his will. Miles does not have the key to unlock the door and the apartment is on the thirty-sixth floor. The windows are, however, open. Has J.P. committed a crime(s)?

Your Answer

_____

_____

_____

_____

_____

_____

Model Answer

J.P. has committed the crime of false imprisonment. To have false imprisonment, there must be an intentional confinement of a person against their will with no reasonable way of escaping. The facts show that Miles was confined against his will. J.P. locked the apartment door intentionally, and, although the windows were open, the apartment was on the thirty-sixth floor and it would be unreasonable to expect Miles to escape by exiting through the window, even though they were open.

The Facts: Part Two

This section is about what happened after Charlotte's suicide. After reading this new evidence, answer the bonus question. Reread the prior facts before starting the bonus question.

Harvard dean of students office—one month later.
Nathan is sitting uncomfortably in a stiff backed chair. Charlotte's parents sit across from him on the couch.
MRS. GAINSWORTH – So how are your parents?
NATHAN – Fine, thank you.
Silence.
MRS. – GAINSWORTH Are they still thinking about moving to Connecticut?
NATHAN – No, I think they're gonna stay in Newton.
Mrs. Gainsworth folds her hands nervously.
MRS. GAINSWORTH – That's nice. And your—
MR. GAINSWORTH – Marion, will you stop chattering!
Embarrassed, she looks to the ground. Mr. Gainsworth turns to Nathan, his cold stare bearing into Nathan's eyes.
MR. GAINSWORTH – She was everything to us.

NATHAN – It wasn't my fault!

MR. GAINSWORTH – You were there.

NATHAN – But I couldn't do anything! If I'd known she was going to.

MR. GAINSWORTH – What would you have done!? Well, you better figure out what you're gonna do now.

Mr. Gainsworth glares at Nathan angrily, but before Nathan can respond, the door opens, and the Dean and District Attorney Michael Pattillo walk in. Everyone stands. The Dean offers his hand to Mr. Gainsworth and his wife.

DEAN – Please excuse me, my other meeting ran longer than I expected.

MR. GAINSWORTH – That's all right.

DEAN – Do you folks know Michael Pattillo? He's the district attorney for Boston.

The D.A. smiles and greets the Gainsworths and Nathan.

D.A. – I believe we met last year.

Everyone sits down.

D.A. – First, let me tell you how sorry I am about your daughter.

Mrs. Gainsworth looks away painfully.

MR. GAINSWORTH – Thank you...

D.A. – Nathan, do you mind telling us what happened that night?

Nathan swallows and begins slowly.

NATHAN – Well, sir, that night I was home alone, and I heard something in the kitchen. It sounded like someone coming in the door. I didn't think it was my roommate because he was supposed to be at a concert.

NATHAN – But I called out anyway, and no one answered. When I went to see what was going on, someone hit me on the head with a gun.

The D.A. nods.

NATHAN – As I fell, I grabbed his arm and pulled him to the ground. We kept on fighting and I tried to knock the gun out of his hand but it went off. Just as the gun went off, J.P. walked in. He pulled the ski mask off the person and then I saw it was Miles and I went into shock. J.P. checked to see if he was still breathing and he said he was dead. I don't remember much after that.

D.A. – So what did you do?

NATHAN – I helped J.P. put Miles in the back seat of the car.

Charlotte's mother wipes her eyes painfully.

NATHAN – Then I went back to the apartment and Charlotte came over. I told her that there had been an accident and that Miles might be dead. She was very upset. That's the last time I spoke to her.

Harvard Dean of Students office—a few weeks later.

Miles is sitting in front of the Dean.

DEAN – This is very painful for me.

Miles sits silently.

DEAN – Detective Morris from the Boston police department is waiting outside.

The Dean shifts uncomfortably in his chair.

DEAN – You're being charged for the death of Charlotte Gainsworth.

Shock comes over Miles's face as he sits numbly in his chair.

DEAN – I'm sorry. But Nathan claims that you were part of a scheme that caused Charlotte to commit suicide. So, unfortunately, the District Attorney has decided to charge you for her death under the felony murder statute.

Miles shakes his head in disbelief.

MILES – That's bull. He's lying. Ask J.P. He'll tell you!

DEAN – Calm down, Miles…

Stairwell in Miles's dorm—later than night.

Miles shoves J.P. against the wall.

MILES – What do you mean you cut a deal?

J.P. – Cool out.

Miles grabs J.P. and forces him over to the railing.
MILES – You must be kidding; my futures at stake.
J.P. tries to resist Miles's grip.
J.P. – I didn't have a choice. They traced the elevator thing to my phone.
MILES – So are you gonna testify against me?
J.P. – No! That was the deal.
Miles lets him go.
MILES – Stay out of my face.

Summer's dorm room—the next day.
J.P. looks out the window despondently as Summer fidgets with her hair and another friend, Christina, sits on the floor.
J.P. – So what are we going to do about Miles?
CHRISTINA – We've got to help him.
J.P. – No kidding.
SUMMER – C'mon guys, we don't have much time.
CHRISTINA – I can call my sister. She's in law school.
J.P. – She probably knows more than Miles's lawyer.
CHRISTINA – I doubt that.
J.P. – Well, guess what? Miles's lawyer is a tax attorney.
CHRISTINA – You're kidding!
J.P. – No. I'm not. Since he can't afford a criminal lawyer, the public defender's office assigned him one.
CHRISTINA – But a tax attorney?
J.P. – Apparently there's a shortage of public defenders so the Massachusetts bar created a lottery system that all lawyers have to participate in.
SUMMER – This doesn't sound good.
CHRISTINA – You don't think he'll go to jail, do you?
J.P. – Not if he pleads, but if he loses at trial, he'll probably get time.

The Trial

Boston Criminal Courts building—six months later.

Aerial view of the courthouse as people begin streaming in. Miles walks in and sits at the defense table with his lawyer, Marino.

On the other side of the room, Patillo, the District Attorney, is already seated and whispering something to one of his assistants.

The jury files in and the noise in the courtroom subsides.

BALIFF – All rise, Oyer, Oyer, Oyer. The Criminal Court for the State of Massachusetts is now in session.

The judge enters and sits, and the courtroom follows.

CLERK – The people of the Commonwealth of Massachusetts hereby bring the charge of felony murder against the defendant Miles Broussard.

The judge turns to the jury.

JUDGE – You have heard the charges against the defendant. You are to pay close attention to the proceedings and to the instructions that I will give you.

You are obligated to apply the facts of this case to the law. If, after doing so, you find that the prosecution has proved its case beyond a reasonable doubt, you must find the defendant guilty as charged.

If, however, you have a reasonable doubt, you must find the defendant not guilty.

JUDGE *(to the District Attorney)* – Are you ready to present your opening statement?

D.A. – Yes, your honor, I am.

The district attorney rises and walks to the front of the jury box.

D.A. – Every act that causes damage to another, obliges him, by whose fault it occurred, to answer for it. Ladies and gentlemen, but for the act of Miles Broussard, Charlotte Gainsworth would be alive. We must therefore see that he *(the D.A. points to Miles)* answers for her death.

We both have an important task today. In my role as the district attorney, I must prove two key facts.

First, that the defendant committed a felony. And secondly, as a result of that felony, a death occurred.

The District Attorney walks to a large pad sitting on an easel facing the jury box. He flips the cover sheet back and reads the underlined text written on the first page.

D.A. – In the Commonwealth of Massachusetts, *the intentional use of force or violence upon a person with a dangerous weapon is a felony.* The felony murder statute applies when in the process of committing a felony someone accidentally dies. *It does not matter if there was no intent to kill or inflict great bodily harm. (No longer reading.)*

Thus, we will show that Miles Broussard faked a murder and committed a felony by assaulting Nathan Scott with a deadly weapon. We will then show by way of a suicide note that Charlotte Gainsworth committed suicide because of his scheme. If you find that Mr. Broussard committed the felony and Charlotte Gainsworth died as a result, you must find him guilty as charged.

The camera pans to Judge Newman.

JUDGE – Is that all, counselor?

D.A. – Yes, your honor.

JUDGE (to Marino) – You may present your opening statements.

The camera pans to Marino who shuffles the papers in front of him and clears his throat nervously.

MARINO – Thank you, your honor.

He gets up a little uncertainly and stands behind Miles.

MARINO – Miles Broussard isn't a criminal and he didn't commit a crime.

He then slowly moves to the front of the jury box as he prepares to speak.

MARINO – First of all, the only person that should be on trial is the D.A. for bringing such a ridiculous case against an innocent man.

The D.A. jumps up to object as Marino continues.

D.A. – Your honor, this behavior is totally out of order.

MARINO – Secondly, if you find Miles Broussard guilty, you'll be committing a crime.

The judge bangs her gavel.

JUDGE – Counsel, approach the bench.

The courtroom rings with a buzz and mild laughter.

Harvard Law Library—same day.

J.P., Summer, and Christina are sitting in the stacks of Langdell, the Harvard Law library, looking at law books.

J.P. – This is Greek.

CHRISTINA – C'mon this was your idea.

Summer sees an attractive law student walk in.

SUMMER – Hold on. I have another idea.

She limps over to him with a brace on her ankle.

SUMMER – Hi. I'm Summer and I was wondering if you could help me find something.

LAW STUDENT – *(smiling)* Sure.

SUMMER – I was looking for the code of criminal procedure.

LAW STUDENT – It's right over here.

The law student pulls the book from the shelf and hands it to her.

SUMMER – Thanks. By the way, would this book have the felony murder doctrine in it?

LAW STUDENT – No. What you need is a horn book.

SUMMER – Right, right, that's the one I'm looking for.

The law student takes it off another shelf.

LAW STUDENT – Here you go. So where are you sitting, maybe I can give you a hand.

SUMMER – Really, well, now that you mention it, I'm sitting right over there.

She smiles as he follows her to her seat.

Boston courtroom—next day.
The coroner is on the stand being questioned by the D.A.

D.A. – Did you have an opportunity to do an autopsy on Charlotte Gainsworth.

CORONER – Yes, I did.

D.A. – Would you please tell the ladies and gentlemen of the jury about your findings.

CORONER – Well, our findings indicated that the cause of death was asphyxiation. There were burn marks around her neck, which appeared to be caused by an electrical cord.

And since there was no evidence of a struggle I would venture to say that she died from self-inflicted strangulation.

D.A. – In other words, suicide.

CORONER – Yes, in my professional opinion I would say that she committed suicide.

D.A. – Thank you.

The D.A. turns to the judge.

D.A. – No further questions.

JUDGE – Mr. Marino, do you care to cross-examine the witness?

Marino rises and walks toward the jury box.

MARINO – Yes, your honor. It's Dr. Macdow, right?

CORONER That's correct.

MARINO – You stated on direct that you did a full examination of Ms. Gainsworth, is that correct?

CORONER – That's what I said.

MARINO – What else did your findings show?

CORONER – Well, she was in excellent health.

MARINO – Okay. Was there anything unusual about her condition at the time of her death?

D.A. – Objection, your honor, the coroner already stated that she was in good health.

JUDGE – Mr. Marino, where are you headed?

MARINO – Your honor, I have Dr. Macdow's report here and it states that Ms. Gainsworth was six weeks pregnant at the time of her death, isn't that correct, Doctor?

CORONER – Yes, that's correct.

A murmur goes through the courtroom. Nathan walks out.

MARINO – No further questions, your honor.

JUDGE – *(to the coroner)* You may step down. Mr. Pattillo, you may call your next witness.

D.A. – Your honor, we would like to call Bill Bowdoin.

Courtroom—later that day.

Bill Bowdoin (expert) standing in the witness box with his right hand up being sworn in.

EXPERT – I do.

D.A. – Mr. Bowdoin, will you please state your full name and occupation for the record?

EXPERT – My full name is William J. Bowdoin. I am a licensed handwriting expert.

D.A. – By whom are you employed?

EXPERT – I have my own company.

D.A. – Your honor, if the defense would agree, we would like to certify Mr. Bowdoin as an expert in his field. Perhaps we could save the court some precious time.

Marino quickly stands.

MARINO – The defense so stipulates.

JUDGE – Let it be noted in the record. You may continue counsel.

The D.A. moves to the prosecution table, removes a piece of paper, and walks to the defense table showing it to Marino. He then walks toward the witness stand and gives it to the expert.

D.A. – Did you have the opportunity to examine this note?

EXPERT – Yes, I did.

D.A. – In your professional opinion as an expert, can you identify from the handwriting who wrote this letter?

EXPERT – Yes. That is the handwriting of Ms. Charlotte Gainsworth.

D.A. – Your honor, if there are no objections, I would like to offer and introduce into evidence Prosecution's Exhibit A.

JUDGE – It is noted in the record. You may continue.

D.A. – Would you please read it aloud.

EXPERT – "I can't bear to live without Miles, Charlotte."

Tears cloud Miles's vision.

D.A. – Your honor, I have no further questions.

The expert stands and walks out.

JUDGE *(to the D.A.)* – Counsel, how many more witnesses do you have?

D.A. – I have three more witnesses, your honor.

The judge bangs the gavel on the desk.

JUDGE – This court will recess until nine thirty Monday morning.

Everyone in the courtroom rises as the judge leaves.

Marino's law office—that evening.

Miles, Marino, J.P., and Summer are sitting in the office.

MARINO – Miles, you're the only one that can make the decision. But I have to tell you, the longer we hold out the harder it's gonna be to get the D.A. to cut a good deal for you.

SUMMER – There has to be some way to get him off.

MARINO – Honey, I wish there was. But the cards are stacked against him.

J.P. – When we were in the library, we found a rule that said if you had tangible evidence that proved that the defendant did not intend to kill the victim, you could use that as a defense.

MARINO – *State vs. Fairchild.* Look, I've done my homework and I wouldn't be telling him to plead if I thought there was a way out. *(Turning to Miles)* If we lose, you could be looking at a ten-year sentence.

Miles looks at J.P.

J.P. – Follow your gut.

Front entrance to the courtroom—next day.

Nathan is seated in the witness stand and the D.A. is in the middle of his direct examination.

D.A. – Now Mr. Scott, you've told us that on the night in question, the defendant broke into your apartment and assaulted you, is that correct?

NATHAN – Yes, it is.

D.A. – And did he assault you with his fist?

NATHAN – No.

D.A. – Well then, what did he assault you with?

Nathan looks directly at Miles.

NATHAN – A gun.

Miles looks at Nathan stony faced.

D.A. – Is this the gun?

The D.A. hands Nathan a gun that has been marked with an exhibit tag. Nathan examines the gun and hands it back to the D.A.

NATHAN – Yes, that's the one.

D.A. – How did he assault you with the gun?

NATHAN – He hit me in the back of the head with it.

D.A. – So, the gash you received on your head was caused by the gun, is that correct?

NATHAN – Yes.

The D.A. hands the gun back to Nathan.

D.A. – Mr. Scott, would you turn the gun over and read to the court the registration number on the back.

Nathan turns the gun over.

NATHAN – It says TF-4.17.58.

The D.A. takes the gun back and hands Nathan a piece of paper.

D.A. – Thank you. Now, would you read aloud what's written on the piece of paper that I've just handed you.

NATHAN – *(reading aloud)* It's a gun registration certificate and the number is TF-4.17.58. Gun owner John Paul Michaels Sr.

The D.A. takes the gun back.

D.A. – And who is John Paul Michaels Sr.?

NATHAN *(bitterly)* – My ex-roommate's father.

D.A. – And who was your ex-roommate?

NATHAN – John Paul Michaels Jr., but we called him J.P.

D.A. – And was J.P. involved in the assault on the night in question?

Miles's lawyer jumps up.

MARINO – Objection. John Paul Michaels is not on trial here and all questions pertaining to his actions on that night are irrelevant.

JUDGE – Objection sustained. Rephrase the question, counselor.

D.A. – Did the defendant know Mr. Michaels?

NATHAN – Yes, they were friends.

D.A. – And would you say, in your opinion, that they were good enough friends so that perhaps if the defendant wanted to play a cruel prank on you, that Mr. Michaels might help the defendant by giving the defendant his gun.

Miles's lawyer jumps up again.

MARINO – Objection your honor, counsel is leading the witness.

D.A. – Your honor, I'm merely trying to establish how the defendant would have obtained the gun.

JUDGE – I'm going to allow the question. You may proceed.

D.A. *(to Nathan)* – You may answer the question.

NATHAN – Yes, in fact I'm sure that Mr. Michaels gave him the gun.

D.A. – No further questions.

The judge bangs her gavel.

JUDGE – Given the hour, the court will recess until tomorrow morning at nine oclock.

The judge bangs her gavel, again. Summer, J.P., and Christina walk up to the bench where Miles is standing.

Summer and Christina hug Miles, who looks pale and numb from the day's proceedings. Marino is stacking up his papers and putting them in his litigation bag.

SUMMER *(to Miles)* – How are you holding up?

Miles forces a smile.

MILES – I'll be okay.

At that moment, a detective passes by and nods curtly to Christina.

J.P. *(to Christina)* – Who was that?

CHRISTINA – Detective Morris. I saw him when he went in to search Charlotte's room.

J.P. – Did he take anything?

CHRISTINA – I think so. But I'm not sure.

J.P. – Let's roll, I just remembered something.

Interior Police Station-day.

An overweight officer hands J.P. a sheet. Summer, Christina, and J.P. begin reading quickly. J.P.'s fingers trace down a column of items.

J.P. – Son of a bitch!

The Trial Question

In the state of Massachusetts, *the intentional use of force or violence upon a person with a dangerous weapon is a felony.*

The felony murder statute applies when in the process of committing a felony someone accidentally dies. *It does not matter if there was no intent to kill or inflictgreat bodily harm.*

Assume the testimony at trial is true and Miles intentionally used a gun to violently scare Nathan, and as a result, Charlotte died because of that overall scheme. Although under the felony murder statute you don't have to prove intent to kill or inflict great bodily harm to find someone guilty of murder, there is case law that creates an exception to this rule.

That exception allows one to assert his or her innocence by presenting a piece of tangible (physical) evidence that would prove that there was no intent to cause harm to the person who died because of the scheme.

You are an assistant to Miles's lawyer. What evidence would you offer in his defense.

Your Answer

_____

_____

_____

_____

_____

The Verdict

The answer is contained in the following facts.

Boston courtroom—a few days later.
Everyone is assembled in the courtroom. Marino has the floor. He is holding a piece of paper in his hand.

MARINO – Your honor, for my first witness I would like to call Detective Morris.

The D.A. jumps up and objects.

D.A. – Your honor, this is a surprise witness. The defense didn't list him on his witness list.

MARINO – Your honor, Detective Morris was an investigating officer on the case and this shouldn't be a surprise to the prosecution.

JUDGE – Mr. Pattillo, I'm inclined to agree with defense counsel.

D.A. – Your honor, if you're going to allow him to testify, we need time to prepare.

JUDGE – Not on this one. Objection overruled. You may proceed counsel.

D.A. – Your honor, may we approach the bench?

The judge hand signals that they may approach the bench.

D.A. – Your honor, this is a major disruption of the proceedings. Mr. Marino had ample time to notify the prosecution that it wanted to call an additional witness.

JUDGE *(to Marino)* – What's going on here?

MARINO – Your honor, I just learned that Ms. Gainsworth's room was searched without a warrant and certain things were taken that may exonerate my client.

D.A. – Counsel, it's the D.A.'s prerogative to search a victim's apartment.

MARINO – But it's also a crime to withhold evidence.

D.A. – Your honor, I don't know what he's talking about; the facts of this case are clear. Ms. Gainsworth committed suicide because she thought her boyfriend was dead. And he committed a felony by assaulting her friend with a deadly weapon. There is no tangible evidence that could disprove that.

MARINO – Your honor, I have compared the police report with the report submitted by the D.A. and they don't match up. I would like to examine Detective Morris to learn about a missing piece.

JUDGE – Okay, I'm going to allow him to testify, but this better be good, counsel.

Detective Morris, who has been sitting in the back of the courtroom, walks up to the witness stand. The bailiff swears him in.

BAILIFF – Do you swear to tell the truth, the whole truth, and nothing but the truth?

DETECTIVE – I do.

The detective sits as Marino begins.

MARINO – Did you have the opportunity to search Charlotte Gainsworth's apartment shortly after her death.

DETECTIVE – Yes, I did.

MARINO – Did you file a report as to your findings?

DETECTIVE – Yes.

Marino walks over to the prosecution table and shows them the piece of paper.

MARINO – Will you identify this piece of paper for the record?

DETECTIVE – That's my report.

MARINO – Will you please read the list of things that were taken from Ms. Gainsworth's apartment.

DETECTIVE – Two letters, a diary, and an answering machine tape.

MARINO – What was on that tape?

D.A. – Objection, your honor that's hearsay.

MARINO – Your honor, that tape has vital information that could clear my client.

JUDGE – Mr. Pattillo, do you know anything about this tape?

D.A. – No, your honor.

The D.A. looks at his assistants as they frantically pull out the evidence list and start going through it.

D.A. – Your honor, may we approach the bench?

The judge motions for the lawyers to approach the bench.

D.A. – Your honor, we haven't had a chance to listen to the tape and we'd like to request a short recess.

MARINO – Your honor, the tape was on the evidence list of things taken from the deceased's apartment. My client's case should not be prejudiced because the District Attorney didn't take the time to listen to the tape.

D.A. – But, your honor.

JUDGE – I agree with Mr. Marino and I will not hold up this court's proceedings because of your incompetence. Mr. Marino, you may proceed.

The attorneys return to their seats.

JUDGE – I will allow the defense to play the tape.

D.A. – But your honor, the tape has not been authenticated.

JUDGE – Exception noted for the record. Mr. Marino, you may proceed.

MARINO – Thank you, your honor.

Marino pushes the button on the tape machine. The sound of Miles's voice fills the room.

MILES – Charlotte, it's . . . Miles. It's about 10:30. I just left Nathan's apartment. He thinks I'm hurt, but I'm okay. Call me and let me know you got this message. I love you.

The courtroom is silent.

MARINO – Your honor, the defense moves that this case be dismissed under *State v. Fairchild,* which held that where there was tangible evidence proving that a defendant had no intent to harm the deceased, the felony murder statute would not apply. Therefore, we move that the case be dismissed.

The judge sits back and looks through somepapers and out into the courtroom.

JUDGE – I have to agree with the defense.

The judge turns to the D.A. and raps her gavel.

JUDGE – This case is dismissed.

These questions were of varying complexity and difficulty. Since except where specifically noted, your answers would not have contained a discussion of possible defenses, the essay question answers were shorter than what you would typically write during a law school exam. However, the variety of questions—essay, true/false, multiple choice—mirrors what you can expect to have during a typical law school exam.

Some arguments in the sample questions were harder to make than others, thus requiring a sound understanding of the crimes. Also required was an ability to make subtle distinctions and to argue the existence of certain crimes even though the elements may not have been clearly present in the facts. Since clear-cut fact patterns providing obvious crimes and answers are more the exception than the rule, it is imperative you be able to argue by analogy whenever your case does not fit neatly into one or more particular category or area.

You also should have been able to determine correctly when crimes did not exist or, as often referred to by law professors, when questions contained "red herrings"—apparent references to crimes, which, upon further analysis, are not present. Several red herrings were included, which, hopefully, you were able to spot. Remember that nearly every exam question, particularly in criminal law, contains some type of red herring or misleading aspect. This forces you to be astute in identifying when something is really a crime.

We hope that the exercises in this book have helped you to understand more clearly what it takes to be successful in law school. We also hope that this book provided you with valuable insight into how one must approach legal problems.

If you did well with the sample questions, you are well on your way to a successful law school career. If you did not do as well as you would have liked, go over what you missed and try to figure out where you went wrong. For some, this exercise may have helped to prove that you have the aptitude and interest to go to law school and to become a lawyer. For others, this may simply show that you need a little more work or, perhaps, that your true interests and strengths lie elsewhere. Whatever the case, persevere and you will be successful!

10 | GLOSSARY OF SELECTED TERMS

The following terms and others will be an integral part of your first-year vocabulary. The courses in which they are most often used are indicated in parentheses. You will hear these terms frequently from day one, so it is worthwhile knowing them before your classes start. Below are short-hand definitions that will help you to begin using them correctly.

Adverse possession: A method of acquiring real property by continuous, open, hostile, notorious, or exclusive possession of property while denying another's rights or claims to that property.

Appeal: A case can be tried by a higher court to review a lower court's decision and law. When such a review is requested, the party is seeking an appeal.

Consideration: A term and concept in first-year contracts; the thing bargained for in a contract or what you receive for doing what is called for in the contract.

Collateral Estoppel (Civil Procedure): Also known as "issue preclusion" or that the issue was previously adjudicated between the same parties in a different cause of action.

Contributory Negligence (Torts): The negligence, or lack of ordinary care of the aggrieved party that, together with the defendant's own negligence, led to the injury.

Defendant: The person against whom relief is sought.

Due Process: Constitutional protection to uphold private rights against arbitrary governmental action.

Estoppel (Civil Procedure): One is prevented from alleging a claim or proceeding contrary to ones previously stated facts or previous actions.

Franchise: A legal right to operate on behalf of the parent owner or franchisor.

Franchisee: The person to whom a right to use property on behalf of another has been conveyed.

Franchisor: The owner of the property who conveys to another (franchisee) a right to use that property.

Hearsay (Evidence): A statement made out of court, yet offered in court, to prove the truth of the out of court statement.

Injunction (Civil Procedure): Relief in equity that prevents the action or activity in question from proceeding, pending further legal review.

Joint and Several Liability (Torts/Contracts): When parties may be sued either separately or together.

Libel: Defamation against a person that is in writing, printed material, pictures, or signs. This is opposed to spoken defamation, which is slander.

Laches (Contracts): A failure to act or to enforce a claim within a reasonable time.

Lien (Contracts/Property): An encumbrance, charge or security interest upon property.

Minimum contacts: A term used in civil procedure to describe the ties that a person has with the forum or jurisdiction where an action is being brought. The court determines whether minimum contacts exist to assert personal jurisdiction over the person (try them in that court).

Petitioner: The person who petitions or files a claim for relief on appeal against another party or respondent.

Plaintiff: The person who brings an action for relief against another.

Pleading (Civil Procedure): The formal statement by the parties to an action of their claims and defenses. They typically include a complaint, an answer, and a counter-claim.

Prima Facie Evidence (Civil Procedure): The evidence as presented is sufficient to establish the existence of a fact or facts.

Respondent: The party who disputes and answers a claim against them on appeal. The person filing the appeal is the petitioner.

Reversed and remanded: On appeal, a court can reverse (overturn) a lower court decision and send the case back (remand) for retrial on the issues identified by the Appellate Court.

Right to counsel: The Constitution provides that every party to a criminal proceeding has a right to an attorney or counsel. That right to counsel is enumerated in the Miranda rights, which must be read to every person who is being arrested.

Ripeness (Civil Procedure): When a matter is sufficiently matured or evolved to enable a legal proceeding to begin.

Res Ipsa Loquitur (Torts): Literally, the thing speaks for itself. Rebuttable presumption that the defendant was negligent based upon proof that the instrumentality causing the harm was in the defendant's exclusive control and that except for the presence of negligence, the accident would not have occurred.

Res Judicata (Civil Procedure): The matter has already been adjudged; a judgment on the matter has already been decided by a court of competent jurisdiction, is conclusive as to the rights of the parties and prevents the bringing of a subsequent action on the same claim.

Respondeat Superior (Torts): The employer, superior, or principal is responsible for the acts of the employee, subordinate, or agent.

Stare Decisis (Civil Procedure): Practice or policy of courts to abide by precedent and to adhere to previously decided cases.

Summary Judgment (Civil Procedure): Rule of civil procedure that permits a party in a civil suit to move for judgment in their favor before evidence is presented if there is no genuine issue of material fact.

Tort (Torts): A violation of a legal duty owed to a person or property, not based on contract rights, that resulted in injury. The area of law that prescribes the duties and appropriate standards of care and behavior for individuals in relationship to one another is known as "torts."

Waiver of rights: A person can waive their due process rights and their right to counsel if it is done voluntarily and knowingly.

Writ of certiorari: A petition from the Federal Court of Appeals to the U.S. Supreme Court to hear a case due to a claim based on the federal Constitution, a treaty, or a federal statute.

11 | AMERICAN BAR ASSOCIATION APPROVED LAW SCHOOLS

ALABAMA
Samford University
Cumberland School of Law
800 Lakeshore Drive
Birmingham, AL 35229
Website: http://cumberland.samford.edu/
Telephone: (205) 726-2702; (800) 888-7213

The University of Alabama School of Law
101 Paul W. Bryant Drive
Tuscaloosa, AL 35487
Website: www.law.ua.edu
E-mail: admissions@law.ua.edu
Telephone: (205) 348-5440

ARIZONA
University of Arizona
James E. Rogers College of Law
1201 E. Speedway
Tucson, AZ 85721
Website: www.law.arizona.edu
Telephone: (602) 621-1373

Arizona State University
Sandra Day O'Connor College of Law
1100 S. McAllister Ave
Tempe, AZ 85287-7906
Website: www.law.asu.edu
Telephone: (480) 965-6181

ARKANSAS
University of Arkansas Law School
1045 W. Maple Street
Waterman Hall
Fayetteville, AR 72701
Website: http://law.uark.edu/
Telephone: (479) 575-5601

University of Arkansas at Little Rock
William H. Bowen School of Law
1201 McMath Street
Little Rock, AR 72202
Website: www.law.ualr.edu
E-mail: lawadm@ualr.edu
Telephone: (501) 324-9903

CALIFORNIA
University of California Davis School of Law
400 Mrak Hall Drive
Davis, CA 95616
Website: www.law.ucdavis.edu/
Telephone: (530) 752-0243

University of California
Hastings College of the Law
200 McAllister Street
San Francisco, CA 94102
Website: www.uchastings.edu/
Telephone: (415) 565-4600

University of California
Los Angeles
School of Law
385 Charles E. Young Drive
1242 Law Building
Los Angeles, CA 90095
Website: http://www.law.ucla.edu
E-mail: admissions@law.ucla.edu
Telephone: (310) 825-4841

California Western School of Law
225 Cedar Street
San Diego, CA 92101
Website: http://www.cwsl.edu/main_v2011_index.asp
E-mail: admissions@cwsl.edu
Telephone (619) 239-0391, Toll Free: 800-255-4252, ext 1401

Golden Gate University School of Law
536 Mission Street
San Francisco, CA 94105
Website: http://www.law.ggu.edu
E-mail: lawadmit@ggu.edu
Telephone: (415) 442-6600

Loyola Law School, Loyola Marymount University
919 Albany Street
Los Angeles, CA 90015
Website: http://www.lls.edu/
E-mail: admissions@lls.edu
Telephone: (213) 736-1001

University of the Pacific
McGeorge School of Law
3200 Fifth Avenue Sacramento, CA 95817
Website: http://www.mcgeorge.edu/
E-mail: admissionsmcgeorge@pacific.edu
Telephone: (916) 739-7191

Pepperdine University School of Law
24255 Pacific Coast Highway Malibu, CA 90263
Website: http://law.pepperdine.edu/
E-mail: soladmis@pepperdine.edu
Telephone: (310) 506-4000

University of San Diego School of Law
5998 Alcala Park
San Diego, CA 92110
Website: http://www.sandiego.edu/law/
E-mail: jdinfo@sandiego.edu (JD) llminfo@ sandiego.edu (LLM)
Telephone: (619) 260-4600

University of San Francisco School of Law
2130 Fulton Street
San Francisco, CA 94117
Website: http://www.usfca.edu/law/
E-mail: lawadmission@usfca.edu
Telephone: (415) 422-6307

Santa Clara University School of Law
500 El Camino Real
Santa Clara, CA 95053
Website: http://law.scu.edu/
E-mail: lawadmissions@scu.edu
Telephone: (408) 554-4361

Southwestern Law School
3050 Wilshire Boulevard
Los Angeles, CA 90010
Website: http://www.swlaw.edu/
E-mail: admissions@swlaw.edu
Telephone: (213) 738-6700

Stanford Law School
559 Nathan Abbott Way
Stanford, CA 94305
Website: http://www.law.stanford.edu/
E-mail: admissions@law.stanford.edu
Telephone: (650) 723-2465

University of Southern California
Gould School of Law
699 Exposition Boulevard, University Park
Los Angeles, CA 90089
Website: http://lawweb.usc.edu/
E-mail: admissions@law.usc.edu
Telephone: (213) 740-7331

Whittier Law School
3333 Harbor Boulevard
Costa Mesa, CA 92626
Website: http://www.law.whittier.edu/
E-mail: info@law.whittier.edu
Telephone: (714) 444-4141; (800) 808-8188
Fax: (213) 938-3460

COLORADO
University of Colorado Law School
2450 Kittredge Loop Road
Boulder, CO 80309
Website: http://www.colorado.edu/law/
E-mail: lawadmin@colorado.edu
Telephone: (303) 492-8047

University of Denver Sturm College of Law
2255 E. Evans Avenue
Denver, CO 80208
Website: http://www.law.du.edu/
E-mail: admission@law.du.edu
Telephone: (303) 871-6000

CONNECTICUT
Quinnipiac University School of Law
Office of Admissions
275 Mount Carmel Avenue
Hamden, CT 06518
Website: http://www.quinnipiac.edu/school-of-law
E-mail: ladm@quinnipiac.edu
Telephone: (203) 582-3400; (800) 462-1944

University of Connecticut School of Law
65 Elizabeth Street
Hartford, CT 06105
Website: http://www.law.uconn.edu/
Telephone: (860) 570-5000

Yale Law School
127 Wall Street
New Haven, CT 06511
Website: http://www.law.yale.edu/
E-mail: admissions.law@yale.edu
Telephone: (203) 432-4995

DELAWARE
Widener Law School
4601 Concord Pike
P.O. Box 7474
Wilmington, DE 19803
Website: http://law.widener.edu/
E-mail: lawadmissions@widener.edu
Telephone (302) 477-2162

DISTRICT OF COLUMBIA

American University Washington College of Law
4801 Massachusetts Avenue, NW
Washington, D.C. 20016
Website: http://www.wcl.american.edu/
E-mail: deans-office@wcl.american.edu
Telephone: (202) 274-4000

Catholic University of America
Columbus School of Law
3600 John McCormack Road, NE
Washington, D.C. 20064
Website: http://www.law.edu/
E-mail: admissions@law.edu
Telephone: (202) 319-5140

Georgetown University Law Center
600 New Jersey Avenue, NW
Washington, D.C. 20001
Website: http://www.law.georgetown.edu/
Telephone: (202) 662-9000

George Washington University Law School
2000 H Street, NW
Washington, D.C. 20052
Website: http://www.law.gwu.edu
E-mail: jdadmit@law.gwu.edu
Telephone: (202) 994-7230

Howard University School of Law
2900 Van Ness Street, NW
Washington, D.C. 20008
Website: http://www.law.howard.edu/
E-mail: admissions@law.howard.edu
Telephone: (202) 806-8000

FLORIDA
University of Florida
Levin College of Law
P.O. Box 117622
Gainesville, FL 32611
Website: http://www.law.ufl.edu/
E-mail: admissions@law.ufl.edu
Telephone: (352) 273-0890

Florida State University College of Law
425 W. Jefferson Street
Tallahassee, FL 32306
Website: http://www.law.fsu.edu/
Telephone: (850) 644-3400

University of Miami School of Law
1311 Miller Drive, #395 A
Coral Gables, FL 33146
Website: http://www.law.miami.edu/
E-mail: admissions@law.miami.edu
Telephone: (305) 284-2339

Nova Southeastern University
Shepard Broad Law Center
3305 College Avenue
Fort Lauderdale-Davie, FL 33314
Website: http://nsulaw.nova.edu/
E-mail: admissions@nsu.law.nova.edu
Telephone: (800) 986-6529

St. Thomas University School of Law
16401 NW 37th Avenue
Miami Gardens, FL 33054
Website: http://www.stu.edu/Default.aspx?alias=www.stu.edu/law
E-mail: admitme@stu.edu
Telephone (305) 623-2310; (877) 788-7526

Stetson University College of Law
1401 61st Street
South Gulfport, FL 33707
Website: http://www.law.stetson.edu/
E-mail: lawadmit@law.stetson.edu
Telephone: (727) 562-7800; (877) LAW-STET

GEORGIA
Emory University School of Law
Gambrell Hall
1301 Clifton Road
Atlanta, GA 30322
Website: http://www.law.emory.edu/
E-mail: emorylawinfo@gmail.com
Telephone: (404) 727-6802

University of Georgia School of Law
225 Herty Drive
Athens, GA 30602
Website: http://www.lawsch.uga.edu/
E-mail: ujajd@uga.edu
Telephone: (706) 542-5191

Mercer University
Walter F. George School of Law
1021 Georgia Avenue
Macon, GA 31207
Website: http://www.law.mercer.edu/
Telephone: (478) 301-2601

Georgia State University College of Law
140 Decatur Street
Atlanta, GA 30303
Website: http://law.gsu.edu/
Telephone: (404) 413-9000

HAWAII
University of Hawaii
William S. Richardson School of Law
2515 Dole Street
Honolulu, HI 96822
Website: http://www.hawaii.edu/law/
E-mail: lawadm@hawaii.edu
Telephone: (808) 956-7966

IDAHO
University of Idaho College of Law
P.O. Box 442321
Moscow, ID 83844
Website: http://www.law.uidaho.edu/default.aspx?pid=65202
E-mail: lawadmit@uidaho.edu
Telephone: (208) 885-4977

ILLINOIS
University of Chicago Law School
1111 East 60th Street
Chicago, IL 60637
Website: http://www.law.uchicago.edu/
E-mail: admissions@law.uchicago.edu
Telephone: (773) 702-9494

De Paul University College of Law
25 East Jackson Boulevard
Chicago, IL 60604
Website: http://www.law.depaul.edu/
E-mail: lawinfo@depaul.edu
Telephone: (312) 362-8701

University of Illinois College of Law
504 East Pennsylvania Avenue
Champaign, IL 61820
Website: http://www.law.illinois.edu
E-mail: llm@law.uiuc.edu
Telephone: (217) 333-0931

Illinois Institute of Technology, Chicago
Kent College of Law
565 West Adams Street
Chicago, IL 60661-3691
Website: http://www.kentlaw.edu/
Telephone: (312) 906-5000

Loyola University Chicago School of Law
Philip H. Corby Law Center
25 East Pearson Street
Chicago, IL 60611
Website: http://www.luc.edu/law/
E-mail: law-admissions@luc.edu
Telephone: (312) 915-7120

John Marshall Law School
315 South Plymouth Court
Chicago, IL 60604
Website: http://www.jmls.edu/
E-mail: admission@jmls.edu
Telephone: (312) 427-2737

Northwestern University School of Law
357 East Chicago Avenue
Chicago, IL 60611
Website: http://www.law.northwestern.edu/
E-mail: admissions@law.northwestern.edu
Telephone: (312) 503-3100

Southern Illinois University School of Law
1150 Douglas Drive, Mailcode 6804
Carbondale, IL 62901
Website: http://www.law.siu.edu/
E-mail: lawadmit@sie.edu
Telephone: (618) 536-7711; (800) 739-9187

INDIANA
Indiana University Maurer School of Law
211 South Indiana Avenue
Bloomington, IN 47405
Website: http://www.law.indiana.edu/
E-mail: lawadmis@indiana.edu
Telephone: (812) 855-9666

Indiana University Robert H. McKinney School of Law
530 West New York Street
Indianapolis, IN 46202
Website: http://indylaw.indiana.edu/
E-mail: lawadmit@iupui.edu
Telephone: (317) 274-8523

Notre Dame Law School
PO Box 780
Notre Dame, IN 46556
Website: http://law.nd.edu/
E-mail: lawadmit@nd.edu
Telephone: (574) 631-6627

Valparaiso University Law School
656 South Greenwich Street
Valparaiso, IN 46383
Website: http://www.valpo.edu/law/
E-mail: law.admissions@valpo.edu
Telephone: (219) 465-7829; (888) 825-7652

IOWA
Drake University Law School
2621 Carpenter Avenue
Des Moines, IA 50311
Website: http://www.law.drake.edu/
E-mail: lawadmit@drake.edu
Telephone: (515) 271-2824; (800) 44-DRAKE, ext. 2824

University of Iowa College of Law
280 Boyd Law Building
Melrose and Byington
Iowa City, IA 52242
Website: http://www.law.uiowa.edu/
E-mail: law-admissions@uiowa.edu
Telephone: (319) 335-9034; (800) 553-IOWA, ext. 9034

KANSAS
University of Kansas School of Law
West 15th Street
Lawrence, KS 66045
Website: http://www.law.ku.edu/
E-mail: admitlaw@ku.edu
Telephone: (785) 864-4550

Washburn University School of Law
1700 SW College Avenue
Topeka, KS 66621
Website: http://www.washburnlaw.edu/
E-mail: admissions@washburnlaw.edu
Telephone: (785) 670-1060

KENTUCKY
University of Louisville
Louis D. Brandeis School of Law
Louisville, KY 40292
Website: http://www.law.louisville.edu/
Telephone: (502) 852-6358

Northern Kentucky University
Salmon P. Chase College of Law
Nunn Drive
Highland Heights, KY 41099
Website: http://chaselaw.nku.edu/
E-mail: chaseadmissions@nku.edu
Telephone: (859) 572-5340

University of Kentucky College of Law
620 South Limestone Street #209
Lexington, KY 40506
Website: http://www.uky.edu/Law/
Telephone: (859) 257-1678

LOUISIANA
Louisiana State University
Paul M. Herbert Law Center
East Campus Drive
Baton Rouge, LA 70803
Website: http://www.law.lsu.edu/
E-mail: info@law.lse.edu
Telephone: (225) 578-5292

Loyola University New Orleans College of Law
7214 St. Charles Avenue, Box 901
New Orleans, LA 70118
Website: http://law.loyno.edu/
Telephone: (504) 861-5739

Southern University Law Center
PO Box 9294
Baton Rouge, LA 70813
Website: http://www.sulc.edu/index_v3.htm
E-mail: vwilkerson@sulc.edu
Telephone: (504) 771-2552
Fax: (504) 771-2474

Tulane University Law School
Weinmann Hall
6329 Freret Street
New Orleans, LA 70118
Website: http://www.law.tulane.edu/
E-mail: admissions@law.tulane.edu
Telephone: (504) 865-5939

MAINE
University of Maine School of Law
246 Deering Avenue
Portland, ME 04102
Website: http://mainelaw.maine.edu/
E-mail: mainelaw@usm.maine.edu
Telephone: (207) 780-4341

MARYLAND
University of Baltimore School of Law
1415 Maryland Ave
Baltimore, MD 21201
Website: http://law.ubalt.edu
E-mail: lwadmiss@ubalt.edu
Telephone: (410) 837-4459

University of Maryland Francis King Carey School of Law
500 West Baltimore Street
Baltimore, MD 21201
Website: http://www.law.umaryland.edu/index.html
E-mail: admissions@law.umaryland.edu
Telephone: (410) 706-7214

MASSACHUSETTS
Boston College Law School
885 Centre Street
Newton, MA 02459
Website: http://www.bc.edu/schools/law/home.html
E-mail: bclawadm@bc.edu
Telephone: (617) 552-4340

Boston University School of Law
765 Commonwealth Avenue
Boston, MA 02215
Website: http://www.bu.edu/law/
E-mail: bulawadm@bu.edu
Telephone: (617) 353-3110

Harvard Law School
1563 Massachusetts Avenue
Cambridge, MA 02138
Website: http://www.law.harvard.edu
E-mail: jdadmiss@law.harvard.edu
Telephone: (617) 495-1000

Northeastern University School of Law
360 Huntington Avenue
Boston, MA 02115
Website: http://www.northeastern.edu/law/
E-mail: lawweb@neu.edu
Telephone: (617) 373-2395

Suffolk University Law School
120 Tremont Street
Boston, MA 02108
Website: http://www.law.suffolk.edu/
E-mail: lawadm@suffolk.edu
Telephone: (617) 573-8000

MICHIGAN
University of Detroit Mercy School of Law
651 East Jefferson
Detroit, MI 48226
Website: http://www.law.udmercy.edu/
E-mail: udmlawao@udmercy.edu
Telephone: (313) 596-0200

University of Michigan Law School
625 South State Street
Ann Arbor, MI 48109
Website: http://www.law.umich.edu
Telephone: (734) 764-1358

Thomas M. Cooley Law School
300 S. Capital Avenue
Lansing, MI 48901
Website: http://www.cooley.edu/
E-mail: admissions@cooley.edu
Telephone: (517) 371-5140, ext. 2244

Wayne State University Law School
471 West Palmer Street
Detroit, MI 48202
Website: http://www.law.wayne.edu/
E-mail: lawinquire@wayne.edu
Telephone: (313) 577-3933

MINNESOTA
Hamline University School of Law
Hewitt Avenue
St. Paul, MN 55104
Website: http://law.hamline.edu/
E-mail: lawadm@hamline.edu
Telephone: (651) 523-2800

University of Minnesota Law School
Walter F. Mondale Hall
229 19th Avenue South
Minneapolis, MN 55455
Website: http://www.law.umn.edu/
E-mail: jdadmissions@umn.edu
Telephone: (612) 625-1000

William Mitchell College of Law
875 Summit Avenue
St. Paul, MN 55104
Website: http://www.wmitchell.edu/
E-mail: admissions@wmitchell.edu
Telephone: (651) 227-9171; (888) 962-5529

MISSISSIPPI
University of Mississippi School of Law
481 Coliseum Drive
Oxford, MS 38655
Website: http://www.law.olemiss.edu/
Telephone: (662) 915-7361

MISSOURI
University of Missour School of Law
203 Hulston Hall
Columbia, MO 65211
Website: http://www.law.missouri.edu/
Telephone: (573) 882-6487

University of Missouri-Kansas City School of Law
500 East 52nd Street
Kansas City, MO 64110
Website: http://www.law.umkc.edu/
Telephone: (816) 235-1644

Saint Louis University School of Law
3700 Lindell Boulevard
St. Louis, MO 63108
Website: http://law.slu.edu/
Telephone: (314) 977-2800

Washington University School of Law
One Brookings Drive
St. Louis, MO 63130
Website: http://law.wustl.edu/
E-mail: admiss@wulaw.wustl.edu
Telephone: (314) 935-6400

MONTANA
University of Montana School of Law
32 Campus Drive
Missoula, MT 59812
Website: http://www2.umt.edu/law/
E-mail: UMSchoolofLaw@umontana.edu
Telephone: (406) 243-4311

NEBRASKA
Creighton University School of Law
2500 California Plaza
Omaha, NE 68178
Website: http://www.creighton.edu/law
E-mail: lawadmit@creighton.edu
Telephone: (402) 280-2872

University of Nebraska College of Law
PO Box 830902
Lincoln, NE 68583
Website: http://law.unl.edu
E-mail: lawadm@unl.edu
Telephone: (402) 472-2161

NEW HAMPSHIRE
University of New Hampshire School of Law
White Street
Concord, NH 03301
Website: http://law.unh.edu
E-mail: admissions@law.unh.edu
Telephone: (603) 228-9217

NEW JERSEY
Rutgers School of Law—Camden
217 North Fifth Street
Camden, NJ 08102
Website: http://camlaw.rutgers.edu/
E-mail: admissions@camlaw.rutgers.edu
Telephone: (856) 225-6375

Rutgers School of Law—Newark
123 Washington Street
Newark, NJ 07102
Website: http://law.newark.rutgers.edu/
Telephone: (973) 353-5561

Seton Hall University School of Law
One Newark Center
Newark, NJ 07102 Website: http://law.shu.edu/
E-mail: admitme@shu.edu
Telephone: (973) 642-8500

NEW MEXICO
University of New Mexico School of Law
MSC11 6070
1 University of New Mexico
Albuquerque, NM 87131
Website: http://lawschool.unm.edu/
Telephone: (505) 277-2146

NEW YORK
Albany Law School of Union University
80 New Scotland Avenue
Albany, NY 12208
Website: http://www.albanylaw.edu/
E-mail: admissions@albanylaw.edu
Telephone: (518) 445-2311

Brooklyn Law School
250 Joralemon Street
Brooklyn, NY 11201
Website: http://www.brooklaw.edu/
Telephone: (718) 625-2200

Columbia University School of Law
435 West 116th Street
New York, NY 10027
Website: http://www.law.columbia.edu/
E-mail: admissions@law.columbia.edu
Telephone: (212) 854-0246

Cornell Law School
Myron Taylor Hall
Ithaca, NY 14853
Website: http://www.lawschool.cornell.edu/
E-mail: rdg9@lawschool.cornell.edu
Telephone: (607) 255-5141

Fordham University School of Law
140 West 62nd Street
New York, NY 10023
Website: http://law.fordham.edu/
E-mail: lawadmissions@law.fordham.edu
Telephone: (212) 636-6000

Hofstra University
Maurice A. Dean School of Law
121 Hofstra University
Hempstead, NY 11549
Website: http://law.hofstra.edu
E-mail: lawadmissions@hofstra.edu
Telephone: (516) 463-5858

State University of New York
University at Buffalo Law School
John Lord O'Brian Hall
Buffalo, NY 14260
Website: http://www.law.buffalo.edu/
E-mail: law-admissions@buffalo.edu
Telephone: (716) 645-2052

New York Law School
185 West Broadway
New York, NY 10013
Website: http://www.nyls.edu/
E-mail: admissions@nyls.edu
Telephone: (212) 431-2100

New York University School of Law
Washington Square South
New York, NY 10012
Website: http://www.law.nyu.edu/index.htm
E-mail: law.jdadmissions@nyu.edu
Telephone: (212) 998-6040

St. John's University School of Law
8000 Utopia Parkway
Queens, NY 11439
Website: http://www.law.stjohns.edu/
E-mail: RSVP@SJULaw.Stjohns.edu
Telephone: (718) 990-2000; (888) 9STJOHNS

Pace University School of Law
78 North Broadway
White Plains, NY 10603
Website: http://www.law.pace.edu/
E-mail: admissions@law.pace.edu
Telephone: (914) 422-4205

Yeshiva University
Benjamin N. Cardozo School of Law
55 Fifth Avenue at 12th Street
New York, NY 10003
Website: http://www.cardozo.yu.edu/
E-mail: lawinfo@yu.edu
Telephone: (212) 790-0200

City University of New York School of Law
2 Court Square
Long Island City, NY 11101
Website: http://www.law.cuny.edu/index.html
E-mail: admissions@mail.law.cuny.edu
Telephone: (718) 340-4210

Touro College
Jacob D. Fuchsberg Law Center
225 Eastview Drive
Central Islip, NY 11722
Website: http://www.tourolaw.edu/
Telephone: (631) 761-7000

Syracuse University College of Law
Office of Admissions and Financial, Suite 340
Syracuse, NY 13244
Website: http://www.law.syr.edu/
E-mail: admissions@law.syr.edu
Telephone: (315) 443-1962

NORTH CAROLINA
Duke University School of Law
Science Drive and Towerview Road
Durham, NC 27708
Website: http://www.law.duke.edu/
E-mail: admissions@law.duke.edu
Telephone: (919) 613-7020

University of North Carolina School of Law
Van Hecke-Wettach Hall
160 Ridge Road, CB #3380
Chapel Hill, NC 27599
Website: http://www.law.unc.edu/
Telephone: (919) 962-5106

Campbell University
Norman Adrian Wiggins School of Law
225 Hillsborough Street, Ste. 401
Raleigh, NC 27603
Website: http://law.campbell.edu/
E-mail: admissions@law.campbell.edu
Telephone: (919) 865-4650

Wake Forest University School of Law
Worrell Professional Center, Suite 2305
PO Box 7206
Winston Salem, NC 27109
Website: http://law.wfu.edu/
E-mail: lawadmissions@wfu.edu
Telephone: (336) 758-5430

NORTH DAKOTA

University of North Dakota School of Law
215 Centennial Drive, Stop 9003
Grand Forks, ND 58202
Website: http://www.law.und.edu
E-mail: admissions@law.und.edu
Telephone: (701) 777-2014

OHIO

University of Akron School of Law
150 University Ave
Akron, OH 44325
Website: http://www.uakron.edu/law/
E-mail: lawadmissions@uakron.edu
Telephone: (330) 972-7331

Capital University Law School
East Broad Street
Columbus, OH 43215
Website: http://www.law.capital.edu/
Telephone: (614) 236-6500

Case Western Reserve University School of Law
11075 East Boulevard
Cleveland, OH 44106
Website: http://law.case.edu/
E-mail: lawadmissions@case.edu
Telephone: (216) 368-3600; (800) 756-0036

University of Cincinnati College of Law
Clifton and Calhoun Streets
PO Box 210040
Cincinnati, OH 45221
Website: http://www.law.uc.edu/
Telephone: (513) 556-6805

Cleveland State University
Cleveland-Marshall College Of Law
2121 Euclid Avenue, LB 138
Cleveland, OH 44115
Website: http://www.law.csuohio.edu/
E-mail: admissions@law.csuohio.edu
Telephone: (216) 687-2304; (866) 687-2304

University of Dayton School of Law
300 College Park
Dayton, OH 45469
Website: http://law.udayton.edu/
E-mail: lawinfo@udayton.edu
Telephone: (937) 229-1000

Ohio Northern University
Claude W. Pettit College of Law
525 S. Main Street
Ada, OH 45810
Website: http://www.law.onu.edu/
E-mail: lawadmissions@onu.edu
Telephone: (419) 772-2211; (877) 452-9668

Ohio State University
Michael E. Moritz College of Law
55 West 12th Avenue
Columbus, OH 43210
Website: http://moritzlaw.osu.edu/index.php
E-mail: lawadmait@osu.edu
Telephone: (614) 688-8212

University of Toledo College of Law
2801 West Bancroft Street, MS 507
Toledo, OH 43606
Website: http://law.utoledo.edu/
E-mail: law.admissions@utoledo.edu
Telephone: (419) 530-2882

OKLAHOMA
University of Oklahoma College of Law
Andrew M. Coats Hall
300 Timberdell Road
Norman, OK 73019
Website: http://www.law.ou.edu/
E-mail: admissions@law.ou.edu
Telephone: (405) 325-4726

Oklahoma City University School of Law
2501 N. Blackwelder
Oklahoma City, OK 73106
Website: http://www.okcu.edu/
E-mail: lawquestions@okcu.edu
Telephone: (405) 208-5337; (866) 529-6281

University of Tulsa College of Law
3120 East Fourth Place
Tulsa, OK 74104
Website: http://www.law.utulsa.edu/
Telephone: (918) 631-2401

OREGON
Lewis and Clark Law School
10015 SW Terwilliger Boulevard
Portland, OR 97219
Website: http://law.lclark.edu/
E-mail: lawadmss@lclark.edu
Telephone: (503) 768-6600

University of Oregon School of Law
1515 Agate Street
Eugene, OR 97403
Website: http://www.law.uoregon.edu/
Telephone: (541) 346-3852

Willamette University College of Law
245 Winter Street SE
Salem, OR 97301
Website: http://www.willamette.edu/wucl/
E-mail: law-admission@willamette.edu
Telephone: (503) 370-6282

PENNSYLVANIA
Pennsylvania State University
Dickinson School of Law
Lewis Katz Building
University Park, PA 16802
Website: http://www.law.psu.edu
Telephone: (814) 865-8900; (800) 840-1122

Duquesne University School of Law
600 Forbes Avenue
Pittsburgh, PA 15282
Website: http://www.duq.edu/law
Telephone: (412) 396-6300

University of Pittsburgh School of Law
Barco Law Building
3900 Forbes Avenue
Pittsburgh, PA 15260
Website: http://www.law.pitt.edu/
E-mail: admitlaw@pitt.edu
Telephone: (412) 648-1490

University of Pennsylvania Law School
3400 Chestnut Street
Philadelphia, PA 19104
Website: http://www.law.upenn.edu/
Telephone: (215) 898-7483

Temple University
James E. Beasley School of Law
1719 North Broad Street
Philadelphia, PA 19122
Website: http://www.law.temple.edu/
E-mail: law@temple.edu
Telephone: (215) 204-7861

Villanova University School of Law
Garey Hall, Room 51
299 North Spring Mill Road
Villanova, PA 19085
Website: http://www.law.villanova.edu/
E-mail: admissions@law.villanova.edu
Telephone: (610) 519-7000

SOUTH CAROLINA
University of South Carolina School of Law
701 South Main Street
Columbia, SC 29208
Website: http://law.sc.edu/
E-mail: usclaw@law.sc.edu
Telephone: (803) 777-6605

SOUTH DAKOTA
University of South Dakota School of Law
414 East Clark Street
Vermillion, SD 57069
Website: http://www.usd.edu/law/
E-mail: admissions@usd.edu Telephone: (877) 269-6837

TENNESSEE
University of Memphis
Cecil C. Humphreys School of Law
1 North Front Street
Memphis, TN 38103
Website: http://www.memphis.edu/law/index.php
Telephone: (901) 678-2421

University of Tennessee College of Law, Knoxville
1505 West Cumberland Avenue
Knoxville, TN 37996
Website: http://www.law.utk.edu/
Telephone: (865) 974-2521

Vanderbilt University Law School
21st Avenue South
Nashville, TN 37203
Website: http://law.vanderbilt.edu
E-mail: admissions@law.vanderbilt.edu
Telephone: (615) 322-2615

TEXAS
Baylor University Law School
Sheila & Walter Umphrey Law Center
1114 South University Parks Drive
One Bear Place 97288
Waco, TX 76798
Website: http://baylor.edu/law
Telephone: (254) 710-1911

St. Mary's University School of Law
One Camino Santa Maria
San Antonio, TX 78228
Website: http://www.stmarytx.edu/law/
E-mail: lawadmissions@stmarytx.edu
Telephone: (210) 436-3011

University of Houston Law Center
100 Law Center
Houston, TX 77204
Website: http://www.law.uh.edu/
E-mail: lawadmissions@uh.edu
Telephone: (713) 743-2100

South Texas College School of Law
1303 San Jacinto
Houston, TX 77002
Website: http://www.stcl.edu/
E-mail: admissions@stcl.edu
Telephone: (713) 646-8040

Texas Southern University
Thurgood Marshall School of Law
3100 Cleburne Avenue
Houston, TX 77004
Website: http://www.tsulaw.edu/
Telephone: (713) 313-4455

Southern Methodist University
Dedman School of Law
3315 Daniel Avenue
Dallas, TX 75275
Website: http://www.law.smu.edu/
E-mail: lawadmit@smu.edu
Telephone: (888) 768-5291

University of Texas School of Law
727 East Dean Keeton Street
Austin, TX 78705
Website: http://www.utexas.edu/law/
E-mail: admissions@law.utexas.edu
Telephone: (512) 471-5151

Texas Tech University School of Law
Campus MS0004
Hartford Avenue
Lubbock, TX 79409
Website: http://www.law.ttu.edu/
Telephone: (806) 742-3990, ext. 273

UTAH
Brigham Young University
PO Box 28000
Provo, UT 84602
Website: http://www.law2.byu.edu/
Telephone: (801) 422-4277

University of Utah
S.J. Quinney College of Law
332 South 1400 East
Salt Lake City, UT 84112
Website: http://www.law.utah.edu/
E-mail: admissions@law.utah.edu
Telephone: (801) 581-6833

VERMONT
Vermont Law School
164 Chelsea Street
PO Box 96
Royalton, VT 05068
Website: http://www.vermontlaw.edu/
Telephone: (802) 831-1000

VIRGINIA

George Mason University School of Law
3301 Fairfax Drive
Arlington, VA 22201
Website: http://www.law.gmu.edu/
E-mail: lawadmit@gmu.edu
Telephone: (703) 993-8000

William and Mary Law School
PO Box 8795
Williamsburg, VA 23187
Website: http://law.wm.edu
E-mail: lawadm@wm.edu
Telephone: (757) 221-3800

University of Richmond School of Law
28 Westhampton Way
Richmond, VA 23173
Website: http://law.richmond.edu/
E-mail: lawadmissions@richmond.edu
Telephone: (804) 289-8000

University of Virginia School of Law
580 Massie Road
Charlottesville, VA 22903
Website: http://www.law.virginia.edu
E-mail: lawadmit@virginia.edu
Telephone: (434) 924-7354

WASHINGTON
Gonzaga University School of Law
PO Box 3528
721 North Cindnnati Street
Spokane, WA 99220
Website: http://www.law.gonzaga.edu/
E-mail: admissions@lawschool.gonzaga.edu
Telephone: (509) 313-3700

University of Washington School of Law
William H. Gates Hall
Box 353020
Seattle, WA 98195
Website: http://www.law.washington.edu/
E-mail: lawadm@uw.edu
Telephone: (206) 543-4078

WEST VIRGINIA
West Virginia University College of Law
PO Box 6130
Morgantown, WV 26506
Website: http://law.wvu.edu/
E-mail: wvulaw.admissions@mail.wvu.edu
Telephone (304) 293-5304

WISCONSIN
Marquette University Law School
Eckstein Hall, #238
PO Box 1881
Milwaukee, WI 53201
Website: http://law.marquette.edu
E-mail: law.admission@marquette.edu
Telephone: (414) 288-7090

University of Wisconsin Law School
975 Bascom Mall
Madison, WI 53706
Website: http://www.law.wisc.edu/
E-mail: admissions@law.wisc.edu
Telephone: (608) 262-2240

WYOMING
University of Wyoming Law School
1000 East University Avenue
Laramie, WY 82071
Website: http://uwadmnweb.uwyo.edu/law/
E-mail: lawmain@uwyo.edu
Telephone: (307) 766-6416

COMMONWEALTH OF PUERTO RICO
University of Puerto Rico School of Law
Rio Piedras, Puerto Rico 00931
Website: http://www.upr.edu/home1200.html
Telephone (809)764-3827

Pontifical Catholic University of Puerto Rico School of Law
Las Americas Avenue Station # 6
Ponce, Puerto Rico 00732
Website: www.pucpr.edu
Telephone: (809) 941-2000

Inter American University School of Law
PO Box 70351
San Juan, Puerto Rico 00936
Website: http://www.derecho.inter.edu
Telephone: (787) 751-1912, ext. 2056, 2013

ACKNOWLEDGMENTS

The authors would like to acknowledge that, but for the undying love of their parents, this book would not have been written. Through great sacrifice and support, we have been nurtured and educated, and for that, we are grateful.

As well, we would like to acknowledge Gene Davidson, Quay Wallace, Esq., George Jones, Bob Chunn, Kathryn Popoff, Gloria Patterson and Charles Tabor for their support and belief in this project. Finally, we would like to thank all of our family and friends who have been a source of inspiration for us to follow our dreams.

Notes